Too Old To Cry

Too Old To Cry

Paul Hemphill

The Viking Press ∾ New York

First published in 1981 by The Viking Press
625 Madison Avenue, New York, N.Y. 10022
Published simultaneously in Canada by
Penguin Books Canada Limited

LIBRARY OF CONGRESS CATALOGING IN PUBLICATION DATA
  Hemphill, Paul, 1936–
    Too old to cry.
    I. Title.
  PS3558.E4793T6   814'.54   80-51776
  ISBN 0-670-72017-8

Printed in the United States of America
Set in CRT Baskerville

Grateful acknowledgment is made to the following for permission
to reprint copyrighted material:
*California Living Magazine of the San Francisco Sunday Examiner and
Chronicle:* "I'll Do the Cooking, Honey, You Pay the Rent" by
Paul Hemphill. Copyright © 1977 by the San Francisco Examiner.
Mayday Music: Portions of lyrics from the song "American Pie"
written by Don McLean, published by Mayday Music and
Yahweh Tunes, Inc., copyright © 1971. All rights reserved.
Peer International Corporation and Southern Music Publishers: Portions of
lyrics from "California Blues (Blue Yodel #4)" by Jimmie
Rodgers. Copyright 1929 by Peer International Corporation.
Copyright renewed © 1957 by Peer International Corporation. All
rights reserved. Portions of lyrics from "Waiting for a Train" by
Jimmie Rodgers. Copyright 1929 by Peer International
Corporation. Copyright renewed © 1957 by Peer International
Corporation. All rights reserved.
Warner Bros. Music: Portions of lyrics from "Let's Do It" by Cole
Porter. Copyright 1928 by Warner Bros. Inc. Copyright renewed.
All rights reserved.

ACKNOWLEDGMENTS

Grateful acknowledgment is made to the following publications in which these selections first appeared:

Atlanta Gazette: "The Grapes of Wrath," "Old Farts"; *The Atlanta Journal:* "Air-conditioned War," "Boosting Betty," "A Certain Satisfaction," "Fast Freddie," "A Flag on the Square," "The Girl in Gift Wrap," "Love, of a Sort," "Mama-San," "Mister Ham's Overcoat," "Off to War," "The Oldest Game," "Policing the Area," "POW of the Year," "Saturday," "Superfan," "Tales of the City," "The Telegram," "Truck Stop," "Welcome Home, Billy Goad"; *The Atlanta Journal-Constitution Magazine:* "The Burglar and the Burglee," "Living Simply is the Best Revenge"; *The Baltimore Sun:* "The Last Move," "The Promised Land," "Father, 43, Does It Again"; *Charlotte Magazine:* "Birthing Babies"; *Country Music:* "Okie"; *Georgia Magazine:* "Hitching," "Wanted: Riters"; *The Miami Herald:* "End of the Rainbow"; *The San Francisco Examiner:* "The Bad Stuff," "Born Again," "John Dillinger, Jr.," "Ex Drops In," "Georgia, Georgia," "Runaway, Age 40," "Sad Lady," "See America First," "Starting Over," "Jerry U-Haul," "Whiskey"; *Southern Voices:* "Quitting the Paper"; *Sport Magazine:* " 'The Big O' Hangs 'Em Up" (originally titled: "How Much is Left of the Big O"), "Good Old Boys Never Die" (originally titled: "A Good Old Boy Shakes Off the Dust"), "Fi$hing for Catfi$h" (originally titled: "The Yankees Fish for a Pennant"), "The Heroes of My Youth," "The Man Who Hit It (#61)," "The Old Grad" (originally titled: "A Football Factory Revisited"); *Today's Health:* "The Late Karl Wallenda."

For Molly Rebecca Hemphill.
May she never be too old to cry.

"They asked [a friend of mine] how he felt after an unsuccessful election. He said he felt like a little boy who had stubbed his toe in the dark. He said he was too old to cry, but it hurt too much to laugh."

Adlai Stevenson

Contents

War

On the Road

The Coast

Home Again, Home Again

Foreword

"You got a job yet, son, or you still trying to write?"
My old man

On sweltering Southern mornings during the last months of the 1970s, in a room I called an office above Findley's Hardware in a decaying inner-city neighborhood of Atlanta, I crawled about a linoleum floor and pored through Allied Van Lines packing boxes in order to flush out the pieces for this book. My publisher had suggested that I put together an anthology of my journalism. For twenty years I had written and published a thousand words a day—as a daily newspaper columnist, magazine writer, novelist, and author of nonfiction books—and to go back over those yellowed clips was to see my adult life flash before my eyes. "Okay, kid, I've found the perfect title," yelped my editor over the phone while I was in this process of picking and choosing. " 'Too Old to Cry.' It's from Adlai Stevenson. Remember when he said, 'I'm too old to cry, but it hurts too much to laugh'?" *This woman,* I said to myself, *has been reading my mail.*

Too old to cry. God knows. All of my life, first as a hopeful baseball player and then as a fidgety young writer, I aspired to be "experienced." I wanted that knowledge that comes only with time. I wanted to experience success and failure. I wanted to know what it is like to be a steelworker, a politician, a hooker, a sports hero, a bureaucrat, a lover turned out into the cold, a soldier stomping through the mud, a drunk, a show-business personality, a father, and all the rest. I learned all of those things, whether vicariously or in person, and abruptly I found myself nearing forty-four years of age and being very tired. "One thing you got to remember, Hemphill," a friend told me when he took the big gamble and struck out for Hollywood to try it as a writer, "we are no longer promising young men."

A woman at a dinner party, during the period when I was spending my days assembling the best of what I guess to be some seven million words of my published writing, reminded me of that fact as the guests glided from group to group and became introduced and idly conversed. "Betty," said the host, with hands gently at the elbows of me and a brightly painted dowager, "I don't believe you've ever met Paul Hemphill." I was, as usual, hung over and wild-eyed. I remember being in what my wife calls my "uniform" of faded jeans and wrinkled T-shirt and white socks and decadent, out-of-style boots, which had been broken in on the day I bought them, five years earlier, by fishing for trout in the middle of a stream in north Georgia.

"Hemphill," she said. "Paul Hemphill."

"He's a writer," said the host.

"Paul Hemphill." She pondered it. "Where do you write?"

"You name it. I've written for it."

She smiled. "Now I remember. The *Atlanta Journal.*"

"Yes'm. There, too."

"So *you're* Paul Hemphill."

"I used to be." I needed another drink.

And then there was yet another night when four of us, each forty and having been around the block, gathered to commiserate. We had strayed on our own to places like Chicago and San Francisco and St. Simons Island and France and Kansas and New York, but we had always come back to our roots in the South. And so here we sat, four veterans in our middle age, in a seedy hillbilly nightclub called the Twilite Club on the fringe of Atlanta in the company of an owner called Mama and a beefy bouncer who wrestles on television and is every bit the stereotype that Mama and we four old farts are. An old fart. *I never was supposed to become an old fart.*

Soon began the parade all of us had thought would be so much fun. Here came a blond hooker. Here came some old boy with a beard and pointy-toed boots and long sideburns and a Coca-Cola belt buckle. Here came two honeys in brad-studded jeans and Dolly Parton hairdos, smacking gum. Here came some lecherous old devil wearing a string tie. But the band was too loud and the music too predictable ("Here's one we like to call the ol' Ex-Lax Song. We call it 'You Got Me Running' "), and it became obvious that we had abruptly become too old for this sort of thing.

And so we slithered off to some Steak & Egg joint after midnight and cried about having finally become Experienced, which is what we had always hoped for, and at two A.M. I found myself waking my wife and telling her that life wasn't fun anymore. I had finally found the answers, and I found them lacking.

Life *isn't* fun anymore. It was fun when I was in my twenties and thirties because everything was new. The first hooker is fun. The first morning awakening in the mountains to all that dew and smoke and howling of animals is fun. That first confrontation with some old wasted drunk on the dark side of town, with all of his life's story, is fun in a perverse sort of way. That first clandestine love affair is fun. That first childbirth is fun. The first new home is fun. The first baseball game is fun. The first Christmas is fun. The first puppy is fun. But then you recognize that the hooker is neurotic; that the mountains are lonesome; that the drunk is a drunk; that the lover has brought her baggage; that babies burp and fart; that first houses need wallpapering and painting; that baseball becomes redundant; that Christmas becomes expensive; that friendly puppies shit on the floor. The repetition sets in, and all of it becomes, reluctantly, boring.

It is, I theorize, a quite normal progression. In the beginning you want to feel everything. You want to become Experienced. You want to get drunk and get laid and spend a night in jail and feel money in your pocket and love and hate and travel and hear and see. You want to feel all of it. So you do all of those things and you become Experienced and then you sit back—now you have those wrinkles around your eyes and those stories to tell and the position of a *learned observer*—and you think, "Is that all there is?" There are no more surprises. That is the saddest part.

No more surprises. A few years ago another old fart—a fellow named Lee Fuhrman, who had been a copy editor and reporter for the *Atlanta Constitution* since Day One—died alone of cancer in a cluttered downtown apartment. It was Lee who once said to a gaggle of wide-eyed "summer interns" some twenty years ago, in a soliloquy he eloquently delivered around one-thirty each morning as we awaited the Five-Star Edition, "Boys, the newspaper is a monster. The monster requires feeding each day. What the monster eats each day is you. One day you will go in to feed the monster and there won't be anything left to feed the monster." It was also Lee Fuhrman who could, at the age of sixty-five, still get excited when he heard police sirens wailing at six o'clock in the morning. I admired and envied Lee Fuhrman. Life, for him, was a breaking news story.

The irony of it is that you spend your youth trying to become Experienced and then, when you have done so, you become cynical. You have seen it all. You retire to reading the old novels you have always read—*The Grapes of Wrath, The Old Man and the Sea*—eschewing the trendy new ones. You find your happiness not in going out juking but in holding hands with the person you have known a long time. You make a separate peace with the things you best understand, whether it be a particular oak tree or an old Guy Lombardo 78 or a ratty copy of Shakespeare, and you settle down under your shawl and into your slippers and you try to make something out of the whole mess. "I have reached the point," one of the old farts said that night at the Twilite Club, "where I appreciate a good piece of cornbread." It helps, I have found, to have a warm cat sitting in your lap. The name of mine is Dixie Lee Box, a cuddly female, named in honor of the randy teenaged protagonist of my novel about a wide-eyed baseball hopeful and his alcoholic forty-year-old manager who has learned too much for his own good.

Suddenly, it occurs to me, many of my generation *have* become Old Farts. We are no longer Promising Young Men. The editors of an underground weekly in Atlanta recently deemed that anybody who was forty years of age didn't know what the hell he was writing about and purged us all. But those people didn't carry the baggage that we carried—the kids, the mortgages, the alimony-and-support payments, the bad credit, the memory of deceased parents, the time Uncle Billy embarrassed the entire family by declaring bankruptcy in '37—and we were at once angry and envious toward these children of the sixties. They are, of course, going to pick up their own baggage as time goes on. They are sure to experience the highs and lows, from child-rearing to divorce and lowered expectations, before they understand the fight.

I am thinking of what Hemingway wrote in the foreword to a collection of his short stories: "In going where you have to go, and doing what you have to do, and seeing what you have to see, you dull and blunt the instrument you write with. But I would rather have it bent and dull and know I had to put it on the grindstone again and hammer it into shape and put a whetstone to it, and know that I had something to write about, than to have it bright and shining and nothing to say, or smooth and well-oiled in the closet, but unused. . . ."

There is no doubt in my mind that my instrument has been dulled and blunted in pursuit of some answers. I'm also struck by the fact that most of my best writing is ultimately sad. It is about lost dreams and excess baggage and divorce, whiskey, suicide, killing, and general unhappiness: a boy who died in my arms, in a bomb crater, while I wrote in Vietnam; an old lady who simply died of loneliness; a young couple with a child, stranded in a bus station; a pathetic kid from Tennessee who messed up a bank robbery in San Francisco.

Life, I have determined, is a pisser. "I'll never get out of this world alive" is the way Hank Williams put it. Perhaps one takes this position when one has seen too much. Surely some of the pieces here, like those written when I was on assignment in Vietnam, today make me pale to know that I could once feel as I did. Inevitably I find myself wondering, Do we use an anthology as a document of how one changes over the years? Or do we try to clean up the old act—revise history—as we go along? I've opted for the former. What happens to me from here on I do not know—I'm forty-four, divorced, a husband and a father for the second time, out of money as usual, becoming more and more of a socialist and an atheist by the day, more cynical than ever—but I *am* still able to laugh and to cry. I *have* been around the block. But I am pleased to feel that I would like to go around it again.

P.H.

Atlanta, 1979

Jocks

*"Look, I know the fine for speedin' through Ros-
well is ten dollars. How many times you reckon
I've paid it, anyway? I'm just givin' you two tens
because I'm gonna be in a hurry comin' back. You
might say I'm payin' in advance."*

Georgia moonshiner/racer Lloyd Seay

T *here is a framed photograph hanging in a long hallway of our house that makes me infinitely sad. The picture was taken during the summer of 1953 in the rolling hills of the southeastern Missouri Ozarks. I was seventeen years old. I had delivered newspapers all fall and winter and spring and had saved enough money to finance my first adventure. I hitchhiked the six hundred miles or so from Birmingham to the Ozarks, standing beside the asphalt roads with a Jackie Robinson bat and a Bob Dillinger glove and a Sears cardboard suitcase, to attend the Ozark Baseball Camp. I digress. But maybe, then, I don't digress. This photograph, which later made the* Sporting News—*they always called themselves the "Bible of Baseball"—shows four kids posing with one Tyrus Raymond Cobb. Ty Cobb is the one in the center, an old man in a bow tie and gabardine slacks and rolled-up shirtsleeves, demonstrating how he once held the bat with his hands several inches apart. The one directly to his right, skinny and crew-cut and scared to death, is young second baseman Paul Hemphill, of Birmingham, Alabama.*

And so baseball is where it began. I am thoroughly mystified over why so many male American writers—from Hemingway to Runyon to Steinbeck— drew their juices from boys' games. It continues to this day. You could do worse than the novel by former wide receiver Pete Gent, North Dallas Forty, *and you could do worse than the memoir of failed Braves pitcher Pat*

Jordan, A False Spring. *Maybe a friend had it right when he talked about my first novel. It is called* Long Gone, *about an aging alcoholic player-manager in Class D baseball and his groupie girl friend and a frightened teenage second baseman, all of them down and out in the bush leagues, dwelling amid kudzu and wooden grandstands and tin fences and lost dreams. "Sports," the friend said. "Sports has all the elements a writer looks for. It's what made* Rocky *a hit movie. You've got all of those wonderful stereotypes: the lonely center fielder, the imperious superstar quarterback, the fanatical coach or manager, the illiterate Chicano shortstop, the greedy owner, the plastic sportscaster, the stunted little Southern stock-car driver getting some sort of weird sexual power from a 427-cubic-inch engine, and all of the others. Face it: Writers* need *clichés. Sport is the ultimate cliché."*

I failed at baseball. I bottomed out after a five-day tryout in Class D and tucked my tail and ran into seclusion. I didn't come out for two weeks, hiding in a back bedroom of some relatives' house in southeast Alabama at the age of eighteen, and I like to say that in those two weeks I put the first stage of my life behind me and was ready to talk serious. But I still wish Ty Cobb were with us and I could motor up the road to Royston, up into those shadowy foot-hills of Georgia, and show him the picture they took of us together when he was the old man and I was the kid.

The Heroes of
My Youth

Birmingham, Alabama

I t was enough to make a man cry. Yes, indeed, quite
enough. In another time, some twenty years earlier,
there would have been a jaunty mob of four hundred red-faced
steelworkers and truck drivers and railroad switchmen lined up at
the four ticket windows—the soot and grease of a day's work still
smeared on their bodies, their eyes darting as they waited to get
inside old Rickwood Field to take out their frustrations on the
hated Atlanta Crackers—but now, hardly an hour before a game
between the Birmingham A's and the Jacksonville Suns, the place
was like a museum. Five rheumy old-timers lolled about the one
gate that would be open for the night. A broken old fellow who
had celebrated his eighty-second birthday the night before sat on
a stool in the lobby behind a podium stacked with scorecards, a
position he had occupied for most of this century, calling out
"Scorecards, get your scorecards" in the same froggy voice I remember from the first day I walked through these turnstiles
twenty-seven years ago. On the cracked-plaster walls, needing a
dusting, were the familiar faded photographs of the heroes of my
youth: Fred Hatfield, Walt Dropo, Eddie Lyons, Red Mathis,
Jimmy Piersall, Mickey Rutner, and, not the least, Ralph "Coun-

try" Brown. In contrast to the 1948 season, when the Birmingham Barons of the Class AA Southern Association averaged more than 7,000 paid fans per game, the attendance on this blustery June night in 1974 would come to exactly 338.

Quickly climbing the musty stairs to the executive offices, I sought out an old acquaintance. Glynn West had been fifteen years old in 1948, the holder of an exalted position in the eyes of the rest of us. On summer afternoons when the Barons were playing at home he walked the two miles from his apartment project to operate the scoreboard and supervise the kids lucky enough to be hired to shag baseballs hit out of the park during batting practice. Now, in his forties, he found himself general manager of a totally different Birmingham club, now called the A's, fuzzy-cheeked chattels of the Oakland A's farm system.

Seated behind a desk adorned with historic baseballs and photographs from the glory days, West wasn't angry at anybody. "We used to get free publicity on the radio and in the papers," he was saying. "It was a civic responsibility to support the home team back then. But last year we had to spend as much as we spent during an entire three-year period in the late forties just to draw twenty thousand people against the million we drew in 1948, '49 and '50."

"Doesn't anybody care?"

"Oakland cares to the extent that every dollar we take in means a dollar they don't have to pay out. They'll call and say, 'Sorry, Glynn, but we've got to take so-and-so from you. We're calling him up to the big club.' What can I say? If it wasn't for Oakland, I guess we wouldn't have a club in the first place. When we were kids and some rain would come up, the fans would jump out of the stands to help spread the tarpaulin on the field. Now only one club in the league even has a tarp. We had to sell ours to help pay some bills." He fiddled with a baseball once signed by a great Birmingham Barons team of the past. "Go find a seat if you want to. There're plenty for everybody. Last year we had a promotion where the first one hundred people through the gate got a free copy of the *Sporting News*. Four people went away mad."

The Birmingham Barons. With the possible exception of the one week I spent in the spring training camp of a grubby Class D club in the Panhandle of Florida during the mid-fifties, no experience in my life has been so profound as my undying awe for the hundreds of fading outfielders and flame-throwing young pitchers and haggard managers who wore the uniform of the Birmingham Barons during the decade covering the late forties and early fifties. It began on the late-August Sunday in 1947 when my old man, a truck driver, announced that we were going to see my first professional baseball game. The Barons, stumbling along then as threadbare members of the old Philadelphia Athletics farm system (they hooked up with the Boston Red Sox the next year), were playing a doubleheader against the strong Dodger-operated Mobile Bears at Rickwood. I fell in love with it all, at eleven years of age, the moment we walked up a ramp and saw the bright sun flashing on the manicured grass and the gaudy billboarded outfield fence and the flashing scoreboard in left-center and the tall silver girders supporting the lights. I would later read that Rickwood was regarded as one of the finest parks in the minor leagues. Nobody had to tell me that. Yankee Stadium could not have been more impressive to me. Taking our seats, we became one with the crowd: hooting at the umpires, scrambling for foul balls hit into the stands, needling the opposition, *oooh*ing when a lanky Mobile first baseman named Chuck Connors towered a home run all the way over the right-field roof (yes, *the* Chuck Connors, "the Rifleman"). Only Ted Williams had ever done that before, my old man told me, and one day I want to meet Connors and tell him about it. The Barons stumbled through a double defeat. The second game was shortened when disgusted fans began throwing their rented seat cushions onto the field at dusk.

From that day on and for the next ten years Rickwood and the Barons became the core of my life. Hurrying to deliver my seventy-eight copies of the afternoon *Birmingham News* (first, of course, I read sports editor Zipp Newman and his account of the Baron game of the night before), I would take the one-hour trolley ride to Rickwood in hopes of arriving early enough to see the players crunch into the parking lot around five o'clock for their pregame ritual. (One day I was stunned to see that a particular favorite was a gaunt chain-smoker.) In those days the big-league clubs played their way up from Florida to begin the regular season, and during one spring exhibition between the Barons and the Red Sox I out-scrambled an old wino for a ball fouled into the bleachers by Walt Dropo, my hero from the previous Baron season who was getting his shot now in the big leagues. It was a ball that we kids in my neighborhood were able to keep in play for the entire summer. We called it the "Baron ball." At night when the Barons were in, say, Little Rock, I would curl up in bed with the lights out and my radio under the covers to hear Gabby Bell's imaginative re-creation of the game; not knowing for some time that Gabby was merely sitting in a downtown studio with a "crowd machine" and constructing his "live" account from a Western Union ticker tape. Occasionally my family would load up the car at dawn with fried chicken and oranges and potato salad and tea and ride over to Atlanta or up to Memphis to root the Barons through a Sunday doubleheader in the lair of the enemy. We always bought box seats next to the Barons' dugout. One time, in Memphis, Barons pitcher Willard Nixon dropped a baseball in my lap because I was the most vociferous Barons fan in Russwood Park.

Nor did the interest wane during the off-season. There was always some Baron news in the Birmingham papers every day of the winter: The Barons had renewed their lease to hold spring training at Ocala; or the Barons had signed a fading major leaguer such as Brooklyn's Marv Rackley or Bobo Newsom; or the Barons had sold a star from the previous season to a big-league club and he was "thankful for the wonderful fans in Birmingham." And then there was the Hot Stove League. Every Monday night in January and February, downtown at the Thomas Jefferson Hotel, a covey of locally bred stars such as Dixie and Harry Walker and Alex and Pete Grammas and Jimmy and Bobby Bragan would lollygag with fans and then watch a color film of the most recent World Series. And, too, you were likely to run into a Baron star on the streets in December—Eddie Lyons driving an ambulance, Fred Hatfield selling suits at Blach's department store, Norm

Zauchin running a bowling alley—for these were the days when a player might settle down with one minor-league club for the five or ten years left of his career.

Looking back, I am convinced that during those years the Southern Association was the best all-around minor league in the history of baseball. The eight towns were paired off into four perfectly natural civic rivalries—Atlanta vs. Birmingham, Little Rock vs. Memphis, Nashville vs. Chattanooga, Mobile vs. New Orleans—and it was, indeed, regarded as one's civic responsibility to support the home team. Twice my old man and I stood for six hours behind a rope in center field with two thousand others (the park seated sixteen thousand then) to shout obscenities at the Atlanta Crackers. The nearest major-league action was in St. Louis. All of the clubs in the Southern Association had strong working agreements with big-league organizations, but they also had a certain amount of financial autonomy. After one particularly successful season, the general manager of the Barons—a feisty Irishman named Eddie Glennon—magnanimously sent a check for five thousand dollars to millionaire Red Sox owner Tom Yawkey "in appreciation for what the Boston Red Sox organization did" to help the Barons.

There simply wasn't anything better to do during summer nights in those Southern cities at that time in American history. There was no air conditioning. There was little television. There were no nightclubs, thanks to the Baptists, and there was scant affluence to create boating and nights at fancy restaurants. And so, in Birmingham and Chattanooga and those other bleak working-man's towns of the postwar South, baseball was the only game in town. Fans passed the hat around the box seats after a meaningful performance to show their appreciation in dollars and cents. Businessmen offered free suits or radios or hundred-dollar bills for home runs or shutouts or game-winning hits. Kids, like young Paul Hemphill, went speechless in the presence of Fred Hatfield the third baseman. Citizens offered the use of their garage apartment, rent-free, to whoever happened to be the Barons' shortstop that year. In this atmosphere the Barons of 1948, with 445,926 paid customers and a total attendance of some 510,000 for seventy home dates, outdrew the St. Louis Browns of the American League.

With infield practice over, Harry Bright stood smoking a cigarette in the runway leading from the playing field to the newly remodeled A's clubhouse while his young players changed sweatshirts and relieved bladders and played fast games of poker. Bright is forty-five now, a baseball itinerant since the day he signed a contract with the Yankees at the age of sixteen. He knocked around the minor leagues for twelve years, hitting .413 one year in the woolly West Texas–New Mexico League, before getting in eight big-league seasons as a utility player. This was his ninth season as a minor-league manager, his second straight with Birmingham. I remembered when he played for a great Memphis Chicks team in the early fifties, a club managed by Luke Appling and stocked with several veterans who had leveled off at Class AA.

"That was '53," he was saying, leaning against a concrete wall in a gold-and-green uniform identical to that of the parent Oakland A's. "I was making three hundred fifty dollars a month."

"How did you feed your family?"

"With a lot of peanut butter."

He flipped the cigarette away. "Actually I picked up a lot on the side that year. You remember that laundry that used to pay two hundred dollars for every home run hit by a Memphis Chick?"

"The Memphis Steam Laundry."

"Right."

"Had their plant behind the center-field fence."

"Right. Well," said Bright, "I hit fifteen homers that year and fourteen of 'em were at home. Somebody said the laundry shelled out twenty-one thousand dollars in home-run money that year. We had a lot of power that year."

Bright's eyes would shine as the old names and stories were passed around. Ted Kluszewski, Jimmy Piersall, Carl Sawatski. The train travel, the horrendous 257-foot right-field fence at Sulphur Dell in Nashville, the wild extravaganzas promoted by entrepreneur Joe Engel in Chattanooga. The low pay, the poor lights, the fleabag hotels, the maniacal fans, the hopelessness of it all. But Harry Bright has, by necessity, quit living in the past. "It's my job now," he said, "to bring these kids along and prepare 'em for the big club. You know. Teach 'em the 'A's way of baseball.' It would be better for them if more people came out for the games, because a crowd gives you an edge and makes you go harder. But people won't buy minor-league baseball anymore. They can see the real thing, the big leagues, on television. What the hell." His club was slumping into last place. Bright pulled the lineup card from his hip pocket and trudged out to meet the umpires. Hardly anyone noticed.

I should have seen the first signs of demise as early as 1950 when my mother came to see my YMCA team play on a dusty sandlot one day and commented afterward that she would rather watch "boys I know" than go to Rickwood to witness "boys from Chicago and places like that," no matter how good the latter were. When the Little League program came along, involving every kid in America with any propensity whatsoever for the game, it robbed the minor leagues of the business from those kids' parents. Those parents were the hardest of the hard-core fans. Then along came television and air conditioning and affluence (and then the Atlanta Braves, in the case of the South), and one day the minor leagues simply died in their sleep.

The state of Georgia once had twenty-two minor-league towns; now it has only three. In 1973, the Southern Association as a whole drew two thousand fewer fans than Birmingham alone drew in '48. This season of '74 there is no radio broadcast of Birmingham A's games, and the baseball writer for the morning paper is the thirteen-year-old son of the sports editor of the *Birmingham Post-Herald*. Rickwood Field is as pretty as ever, although some of the uncovered bleachers have been taken down. These bleachers were once called the "nigger bleachers," and it was below them that a precocious teenager named Willie Mays once made incredible catches for the Birmingham Black Barons of the Negro American League before baseball finally desegregated. Now high-school football and baseball games share billing with the A's on the lush green turf of Rickwood where once Eddie Lyons and Walt Dropo and Gus Triandos and Country Brown and hundreds of my other youthful heroes trod.

One of the most prominent billboards lining the outfield fences at Rickwood these days is one reading WHEN VISITING ATLANTA SEE THE BRAVES. As the game went on that night, Harold Seiler squinted out to left field and tugged at his A's cap and patted the knee of his wife, Mabel, sitting beside him in their third-base box seats, not knowing quite what he could add to the story of the death of the Birmingham Barons. Hal Seiler owns a paint store in Birmingham and has been known, as long as anybody can remember, as the city's number-one Baron booster. Nearly every night of a Birmingham home game for some three decades, he and his wife have been there. One night last year he suited up and actually managed the A's through one of those insufferable late-season "let's get it over with and go home for the winter" exercises.

"Coached third base, even changed a pitcher," he said.

"You win?"

"Won it, four to one. Bright panicked and took his job back."

Minnie Minoso's son, a fine-looking Kansas City prospect playing right field for Jacksonville, cut down a runner trying to go from first to third and got applause from the Seilers. A black dude in the grandstand behind Seiler began a funky dance in the aisle, wildly thrashing about in a cream-colored suit. "Cat comes every night, too, wearing a different outfit every night. Hell, I bet I know the first name of two hundred of these people. It's like a family reunion out here."

"Zeb Eaton. You remember Zeb Eaton?"

"One that got beaned."

"What year?" I said. Trivia now.

"Nineteen and forty-seven."

"You here that night?"

"Here? Rickwood? I was always here."

"Zeb Eaton."

"Me and Mabel were right here. We heard the thud of the ball hitting his head. Ballpark sounded like a morgue. I helped pass the hat and raise money for Zeb's hospital bill."

I said, "Joe Scheldt. You don't remember Joe Scheldt."

"Joe Scheldt," said Hal Seiler. "Crazy. Absolutely bananas. Fast as a rabbit, though. Let me give you one. I remember 'em all. I bet you don't remember Edo Vanni." I told Seiler that I certainly did remember Edo Vanni, an outfielder who passed through briefly as a Baron. Seiler was crestfallen. "I didn't know anybody remembered Edo Vanni," he said. "As a matter of fact, I didn't know anybody remembered the Barons." A pinch hitter named Pickle Smith was announced for Jacksonville. "Pickle," yelped Seiler. "*Pick*-le. Hey , that ain't no pickle, that's a gherkin. C'mon, you gherkin, back in the bottle. Let's show the Gherkin something out there. . . ." The last true baseball fan, Harold Seiler, of Birmingham, Row Five, Box AA, Rickwood Field, smiled like a cherub as Pickle Smith struck out on three straight pitches.

Superfan

Atlanta

The way Johnny Applegate puts it, the whole thing began while he was still drinking milk out of a bottle and they had the New York Yankee games on the radio. That was a pretty long time ago, but he swears that is the way it started. Then he got this job in New York City, and it was a snap to see the Yanks whenever they were in town. By the middle '40s you could ask Who around here is a Yankee fan? and there was a very strong likelihood that Applegate would stand up and punch you in the nose if you did not like it. But the final chapter, the last straw, came not too long ago when Casey Stengel left his false teeth behind at the hotel where Applegate worked and Applegate returned them, thereby consummating his marriage with the Yankees.

This Applegate is a big nut for the Yanks. There was this day in April when they were coming to town for a three-game series against the Braves. Applegate was at the hotel with all the other Yankee lovers waiting to get a glimpse of their heroes, and he was talking to the guy standing next to him.

"Yeah, they call me the 'number-one Yankee fan,' " says Applegate.

"I know a guy who'll dispute that," this guy tells him.

Applegate's hair stood on end. "Who?"

"Guy in Jacksonville. He's the Yank fan of the world."

Applegate snapped, "I'm not claiming the world. Just Georgia."

A funny thing happened this summer. Applegate, the way it used to be, was always calling up or coming down in person to the sports department and hanging around and asking questions like How long before the Yanks clinch the pennant? and When does the World Series start? We do not see Applegate hanging around so much anymore, and when he does make an appearance it is to talk about the Falcons or to inquire about Braves tickets. He does not wish to discuss the Yankees anymore. Very unusual. Everybody else has been talking about them since they landed in last place in the American League.

It has been a bad year for New York City. You had the blackout, no water, no transportation and virtually no newspapers. New Yorkers, being what they call hardy city types, were somehow prepared for all these failures. But nobody was prepared for the collapse of the Yankees.

The last time the Yankees finished in the American League cellar was in 1912. Since then they have had a corporate image that even Coca-Cola would be proud of. They have won twenty-nine pennants, fourteen of them in the last seventeen years. They had farm clubs that could have finished in the first division of the American League. Casey Stengel could pull on his right earlobe and a guy would hit a home run and they would call Stengel a genius for calling the right move at the right time. All they had to do to sign a kid without shelling out a bonus was let him take one look at Yankee Stadium.

And what this caused was the most obnoxious sports fan the world ever suffered. Everybody was a Yankee fan. Little old ladies would lie about being sick just to stay home and watch the Yanks take four in a row in the Series. You couldn't get a bet on the Yanks in the Series unless you put up your house against a couple of bucks. It was the easiest thing in the world, being a Yank fan. It was like betting on a one-horse race.

Hah. Move around a little and see where the Yankee fans are

today; where they were Friday, when the American League standings showed New York holding up the rest of the league, twenty-nine full games out of first place and a whole game back of a bunch of patsies like the Washington Senators, if you can believe it. And where were they Thursday afternoon, when the Yanks played the White Sox at Yankee Stadium and 413 (four hundred and thirteen) bothered to show? A lot of subway cars did that good in ten minutes.

Friday, Applegate is eating his heart out. He drops by the sports department wearing a pinstriped blazer and trying to act like nothing has happened, but it doesn't work. He is not fooling anybody.

"What happened to the Yanks?" I ask him.

"Great night for the Braves game," he says.

"What about the Yankees?"

With a straight face Applegate says, "Wait till next year."

Hah. Beautiful. Fifty-four years we've been waiting to hear it.

The Man Who Hit No. 61

Gainesville, Florida

The only time I had seen the man in person was on a bright Sunday morning during spring training of 1964, at Al Lopez Field, in Tampa, while the New York Yankees took batting practice before an exhibition game against the Cincinnati Reds. This was when the Yankees were still the Yankees—Clete Boyer, Elston Howard, Jim Bouton and Whitey Ford, and, of course, Mickey Mantle and Roger Maris—during that period when it didn't matter who the manager was. They had won the American League pennant by a laughable 10½ games the year before, winning 104 games, and there was no reason to think anybody was yet capable of heading them off.

Even while the Yankees took batting practice there was a murmur in the air, extremely rare for the exhibition season, because this was a club with electricity at each position. It wasn't only in the stands. It was also on the field where two dozen writers and broadcasters swirled about the batting cage. They wanted something new about Mantle's knee, which had endured only 172 at-bats the year before. They wanted something witty or obscene from Joe Pepitone and new manager Yogi Berra. Most of all, though, they wanted anything they could get out of Roger Maris, who had become a swell, many of the New York writers wrote, since hitting sixty-one home runs three seasons earlier to break the most important sports record of the twentieth century. Roger Maris had beaten Babe Ruth.

Grim, unshaven, Maris strode out of the dugout that morning with a bat in one hand and a glove in the other. Every newsman turned toward him. He looked like a man headed to the gallows. His fierce green eyes sank into hollow ringed sockets. "Hey, Rog, show us your asterisk," one of the New York writers said. This was a cruel reference to Maris's having had eight more games in which to reach sixty-one homers than Ruth had. The remark drew nervous laughs. I don't know whether Maris flinched, or if he even heard it, but as soon as he reached the cage his teammates mercifully stepped aside until he could get in all of his licks at one turn. When he finished he bolted to deepest center field until batting practice was over. I had read him described as "sullen" and "arrogant" and "surly." But he seemed more to be a man who was thoroughly unhappy with his work and anybody connected with it. The man, clearly, was tired of all this racket.

A decade later, as another generation of players began to report for another spring training, I had no idea what to expect as I waited at the bar of a glassy new motel in Gainesville to talk with Roger Maris about hitting home runs and coping with pressure and his own retirement from baseball. I had heard varying stories—that he was drinking, that he was still bitter about baseball, that finally he had found some peace of mind—and I was flabbergasted when he quickly agreed to an interview with a perfect stranger ("I guess you just caught me at the right time").

At any rate, at a little before six o'clock in the afternoon he walked briskly into the Taverna Lounge—it is one of those modern motel bars humming with bouffanted secretaries and Jaycees stopping off after work, and a place frequented by Maris—and to me there was absolutely no connection between Roger Maris at thirty-nine and the one whose hair had started falling out at the age of twenty-six from the pressure of trying to break Babe Ruth's record. He was impeccably dressed in a wine-colored blazer and blue shirt and flared gray trousers and paisley tie. His face was

bronzed and healthy. He was smiling, and before he could order a
Michelob he was being warmly greeted by an array of other successful men-on-the-go—the smiling Greek who runs the place, a
college professor, a young University of Florida football coach—
who did not fawn over him but rather treated him as merely a nice
fellow who happened to be a friend. "I'll talk about anything," he
told me with an *Aw, shucks* grin, "except 1961, Babe Ruth, Henry
Aaron, Tracy Stallard, pressure, and New York. Anything you
want to know about the beer business, I'm all yours. Shoot."

It would occur to me rather quickly that Roger Eugene Maris is
one of those rare athletes for whom life began, rather than ended,
with retirement. "Baseball was never any fun for me after I hit the
sixty-one," he said. "The fans and the writers wanted me to go
around acting like Babe Ruth, Jr., but he and I had different
styles. If only it had been possible to play under one name and live
under another, maybe it would've worked out." After averaging
more than thirty-six homers a season during his hottest five-year
stretch with the Yankees, he hit a total of only thirty-five in his
final four seasons at New York and St. Louis. He retired at thirty-
four after his 1968 season with the Cardinals. With the help of
Cards owner Augie Busch he bought into the Budweiser eight-
county beer distributorship based in northern Florida and determined that finally, if he were lucky, he would be able to find the
anonymity he had always wanted. He would play golf, raise his six
kids, eat his wife's home cooking, and simply become somebody's
neighbor. Miraculously, because Maris was so determined to
make it that way, the plan has worked. He occupies his time with
golf, tennis, swimming, and helping his brother operate what is
surely one of the most successful beer distributorships in the country. His weight is about 225, some twenty pounds over his playing
weight ten years ago, and his hair has grown back full. He has
been asked many times to join the mainstream of civic boosters in
one form or another—Gainesville is the home of the University of
Florida—but the answer is always that he wants to be left alone.

A man who came out of the provinces of Fargo, North Dakota,
and hated the city of New York with a passion—for eleven of the

twelve years he was in the major leagues he kept his family in Independence, Missouri—Maris adamantly refuses to play the part
of the once-great baseball star, *the Man Who Beat the Babe.* He has
played in only one old-timers' game, that in St. Louis a couple of
years ago, solely as a favor to Augie Busch. He saw Mantle that
day, and he recently bumped into Clete Boyer in Atlanta, and this
spring he thought he would take his four boys down to St. Peters-
burg to see his good pal Mike Shannon (now a Cardinals broad-
caster) and let the boys watch a day or two of spring training.
Always the type to manage his income frugally—at his peak he
made $75,000 a year—he lives comfortably in a brick suburban
ranch-style house and is "not a pauper but . . . sure not wealthy."
When he visited Atlanta last season and took in a Braves game, he
met Aaron and agreed to a press conference. That was the extent
of his involvement in the Ruth-Aaron-Maris story as Aaron inexorably drove toward breaking Ruth's career home-run record of
714.

Although he spent a dozen years in the majors with four different clubs, Maris had a career that burst like a comet and made
him a star during the first three years of the 1960s, when he hit
thirty-nine, sixty-one, and thirty-three homers consecutively. In
most of the other years the kid from Fargo was more or less average.
He was all right in the outfield, with a strong arm and average
speed, and the only way he can explain his sudden but brief spurt
as a super power hitter is that he "got into a groove there for a
while."

Prior to joining the Yankees in 1960, Maris had spent three
years in the big leagues, with the Indians and then with the Kansas City Athletics, following a mildly promising but erratic four-
year internship in the minors. With Cleveland during his rookie
season he hit 14 homers in 116 games with a .235 average. The
next year, when he was traded early in the schedule to Kansas
City, he totaled 28 home runs in 150 games. He homered 16 times
at Kansas City in 1959 and then joined the Yankees for the '60
season. It was a great club then, embarking on a run of five

straight pennants, and no doubt his being in the company of such players as Mantle had its effect. In his first season with New York, Maris suddenly blasted 39 homers and gave the club a great power tandem.

Roger Maris was already discovering, however, that he was not geared to the special kind of pressure facing the sports hero in New York City. There is the unremitting attention of the fans and the media. Joe Namath thrived on it. The attention made Namath's life go. But Maris, basically a private man who preferred to be fishing or playing golf, felt the world was on his back. "I loved baseball," he says, "and every minute I'm out there in a uniform I'm in my own special world. You have to be like that to play. You have to be able to shut everything else out. I never felt any pressure anytime except when I was playing in All-Star games, and I don't know why that was. It wasn't the pressure of playing. It was the other stuff." He went into a shell and got a reputation for surliness. "I used to go down two or three times a week and have breakfast at the Stage Deli with Jimmy Cannon [the late New York sports columnist]. We enjoyed each other. I liked him. But then one morning, either during or after the '61 season, he comes in and starts to sit down and I tell him, 'Not today, Jimmy. Please. I got things on my mind.' The next day he rips me. Says I'm an ingrate and I owe my life to the fans. I just simply wanted my privacy."

He had a mediocre spring training in 1961, he recalls, and hit his first home run in the eleventh game of the season. But then, suddenly, the homers came in droves. So did the attention. "I was a wreck when we went into the last week. I tell you the truth, I didn't much give a damn about the record at that point. I wanted to get the season over and go home. I'd never been so tired in my life. When I had sixty I sat out a game in Chicago—the only one I missed all year—before we went back to New York for those last two against the Red Sox." Tracy Stallard happened to be on the mound, pitching his best game of the year, when Maris drilled a waist-high fastball out of sight for No. 61 and the place exploded. "I honestly don't remember having any thoughts when I went around the bases except, 'Thank God it's over.' Now I could go back to Independence and hide. Those guys would have to go a long way to butt into my life again. At least for a few months." As Maris and I spoke, Tracy Stallard was avoiding his past—and his present—in an undisclosed Kentucky Valley town near Cincinnati. The ghost of Babe Ruth haunts them both.

Now Maris and I sat in the dining room adjoining the motel bar, mopping up a big dinner and smoking cigars. Except for the earlier meeting with golfing buddies at the bar, Maris had seen no one come over to pester him, and no heads had turned his way. In addition to the New York press, he was saying, he had also been in trouble with Yankee general manager Ralph Houk. "He kept saying I was dogging it one year [1965, when he played in only forty-six games, owing to a hand injury], and he was making me pinch-hit when I couldn't even swing the bat in the on-deck circle. He calls me in the last week and says, after I've had some X-rays made, 'I might as well tell you that you've got to have surgery.' He didn't even apologize." He told the Yankees they could either trade him or he would quit, and after the 1966 season, during which he hit .233 with 13 homers in 119 games, he was traded to St. Louis. Even though he muddled through two seasons there, hitting a total of fourteen homers, he enjoyed playing for the Cardinals' two pennant winners. "I'll always regret that I didn't have my good years in St. Louis, rather than in New York."

Maris was asked if he could relate to Henry Aaron, only two away from breaking the all-time home-run record of Ruth, as spring training got underway. "Henry's got a different kind of pressure," he said. "He's got a whole year to hit two home runs. Hell, last year he hit forty. From what they tell me about him he won't let pressure get to him." Ordering a Michelob to wash down his dinner, Maris seemed to let his mind wander for a minute or two. He asked where Tracy Stallard was these days. When told Tracy was having some problems, he said he was sorry to hear it. "It's tough, being remembered for throwing Number Sixty-one, but I guess it works both ways. It was tough for me, too, *hitting* Number Sixty-one. I made a little money on endorsements after that season, but I'll bet I turned down more chances than I accepted. Hitting those sixty-one home runs had to be the most important thing I ever did in baseball. But it also brought me the most misery."

The Late Karl Wallenda

Rock Island, Illinois

E arly on a crisp March morning inside the bleak granite armory at Rock Island, hard by the Mississippi River, they were busily setting up for the opening night of the annual Quad Cities Sports, Boat, Camping, and Vacation Show. The cavernous hall was a jungle of new boats and campers being preened and drawn into place by proud exhibitors while workmen swept out the grandstand and dumped trout into an artificial pond and finished nailing up exhibition booths. Still, the entire scene was dominated by one thing: *the wire*. The show would run for five days and would draw thousands of outdoor enthusiasts, resulting in many sales for the exhibitors, and the main attraction—"the hooker," as promoters are wont to say—would be the appearance of the famous Wallenda high-wire troupe. Every night at nine o'clock, and at matinees on Saturday and Sunday, ageless Karl Wallenda and the other three—a dusky Chilean named Luis Murillo and Karl's grandchildren Tino and Delilah—would squeak their resined slippers across the fifty-foot cable some forty feet above the concrete floor without the insurance of a safety net. A couple of weeks earlier at a Shrine circus in Madison, Wisconsin, the act had attracted seven straight sellout crowds of nine thousand each in three days, so the Wallendas were expected to move a lot of merchandise for the four thousand dollars they were being paid.

The wire was already up when Karl Wallenda wandered into the building at mid-morning. A dapper, broad-chested man with his mouth stretched in a perpetual sardonic grin, he had already purchased an elegant white-on-white dress shirt and ordered a $110 red blazer, which he would pick up later in the day. "Too bad I don't have it for the television interviews," he said, peering up at the half-inch cable and then mounting the steps to the stage, where Tino sat cross-legged on the floor, braiding a rope. Tino had begun putting up the wire the day before, upon arrival from a circus date in Lansing. Assured that the wire was solid, that the guy wires were taut and the two platforms were steady, Wallenda left the stage and began loitering around the floor beneath the wire as nonchalantly as if he intended to be a spectator rather than a participant that night. "I don't have to check out the wire," he said, "because I have complete faith in Tino. After all, he is going to have to walk on it, too." There is never anything to be afraid of, he said, if you know what you are doing.

It was all very casual until one of the workmen passed by and chirped, "Hey, Mr. Wallenda, you gonna do that dangerous one tonight?"

"They are *all* dangerous," Wallenda said.

"Naw, I mean the one that killed all them people."

"You talk about the Seven-Man Pyramid."

"Yeah. The one with all the people on top."

Wallenda stiffened as he always does when the subject of the Seven-Man Pyramid comes up. It had been his dream stunt and the one he had worked toward all his life—seven people in a precarious three-layer pyramid on the wire at one hundred feet, without a net—but in Detroit's Cobo Hall one of them wavered and they came crashing down. A nephew and a son-in-law died, an adopted son was paralyzed for life, and Karl himself suffered a broken pelvis and a double hernia. The memory is so painful that Karl doesn't like to be reminded of it. "No," he mumbled to the workman, "we don't do the pyramid anymore. There are only four of us remaining." He was glum and distant for the rest of the morning.

Karl Wallenda has lived with fear and tragedy for most of his sixty-eight years. Born into a circus family in Germany, he has been walking the high wire for fifty-two years. In that time he has done many spectacular things—the most noteworthy being an eleven-hundred-foot walk across a treacherous, wind-swept eight-hundred-foot-deep gorge in the Appalachians of northeast Georgia—and consequently he has been celebrated as few performers have been in the history of the circus. Ask the man on the street to recite some famous circus names and he will likely be able to come up with only three: Clyde Beatty, the animal trainer; Emmett Kelly, the clown; and Karl Wallenda, the high-wire artist. For risking his life on the high wire in any number of improbable ways, Wallenda has received as much as ten thousand dollars a crack and virtually transcended the narrow world of the circus.

But he has had to pay his dues. The first tragedy occurred in 1936 when Karl's youngest brother bicycled across the wire at an amusement park in Sweden but was thrown to his death by the high winds. Then came the 1962 Detroit accident, the most celebrated of them all, and three years later a sister-in-law was killed during her own high-pole act in Omaha. And finally, last summer, in Wheeling, West Virginia, his daughter's husband touched an exposed electrical clamp and fell seventy feet to his death. Now the scars on the sprawling Wallenda family, most of them clustered around the patriarch in Sarasota, are unerasable. His wife, who quit the circus fifteen years ago, refuses to watch a performance. Hermann, the oldest brother, was never the same after Detroit and quit two years later. Jana, a niece terrified and almost killed at Detroit (Karl dangled from the wire by his legs and held her for nearly ten minutes until they could get a fireman's net under her), promptly quit and went back to Germany to work as an usherette in a theater. The son, Mario, paralyzed and bitter, inspects contact lenses in a Sarasota laboratory and sees his parents only two or three times a year. Now Karl performs with yet another generation of Wallendas, his two grandchildren, and the possibility that they, too, might be injured or killed weighs heavily on him these days. "Rather than worry about them," he says, "I would prefer to work by myself."

It is difficult to get out of him the reasons why he continues. Five years ago he tried to retire, to turn the act over to the rest of the family, but he went stir-crazy and returned after four months. "I guess it is—what do you call it?—ego." He says he has to do it. "I need to be up there on the wire, entertaining the people and hearing them applaud." On fear and the dangers involved in the act, which has never been done with a net, he is stoical: "It is dangerous. I know that. But the percentages are not that bad. Only one time has death come to the Wallenda family on the high wire. That was Detroit. Wheeling was not a fall. It was a crazy electrical clamp. We have walked thousands of times with only one fatal accident." Does he, the Great Wallenda, become frightened before a performance? "Sometimes, yes, on the night before. Once I have taken the first step onto the wire I am thinking only of getting to the other side. I tell you one thing, and this is no publicity or anything," he says, his steel-blue eyes going blank. "I have one belief, that there is a God in the world. I believe that God stands by you. So anytime I go on the wire I'm not alone. Every night I go to bed and I thank the good Lord that I still have the energy and can still do things. Then, when I have walked the wire, I have two strong martinis and I forget it."

Those around Wallénda have their own theories about what makes him go. "He is a ham, like all of us," says his daughter, Carla, who continued to perform on the high pole after her husband was electrocuted at Wheeling. Karl, says older brother Hermann, "is afraid of dying in bed. He will go until he can't walk. It is ego, no doubt about it." To Jack Leontini, a longtime confidant who lives in the Wallenda backyard cottage and manages Karl's affairs, Wallenda knows no fear. "With Karl it is dedication," he says. "He knows he can walk any wire, anywhere, so there is no need to be frightened. He knows that if he concentrates on the job at hand and walks across the wire, he will receive the accolades that he needs." But to Mario, the crippled son, the reasons his father walks the wire are less mystical. "He knows what could happen, but he doesn't let it bother him, because it is the only thing in life for him. What else could he do for a living?"

Fear is one of our most elusive emotions, one that is often buried in the subconscious, and it is doubtful that there has ever been a truly "fearless" human being in the history of the world. All of us have our private fears—of dogs, snakes, sex, social incompetence, heights, suffocation—which force us to face up to some sort of trauma, large or small, nearly every day of our lives. The truck driver can meet death at any curve on the open road. The young mother lives with the fear of finding her baby has suffocated while taking its nap. The honeymooner worries about his or her first sexual performance; the aging libertine, his or her last. The ways of coping with our fears are myriad: Some psych themselves out of it, whereas others study their anxieties and conclude there is no reason to be fearful. But cope we must, however mundane the fear may be, or forever be haunted by hidden devils.

Then there are those who consciously put themselves in high-risk situations, actually challenging fear and danger: the automobile racers; the stunt men, like Evel Knievel; the sky divers; the test pilots; the hard hats who walk precariously along high steel girders. "You could probably call it a 'counterphobic experience,'" says Roy Grinker, Sr., M.D., a psychiatrist at Chicago's Michael Reese Medical Center. "They take these risks to show others they aren't afraid. Even if they do know fear, they're trying to prove they aren't afraid." And there is another, more fascinating angle. "This fighter pilot, General Robert Scott [a World War II P-40 ace who authored *God Is My Co-Pilot*], wrote something about how after a while the fighter plane actually became an extension of the body." Indeed, when a group of Royal Air Force pilots were interviewed after flying the racy little Spitfire, to a man they described it as a sensuous experience—exhilarating, terrifying, almost erotic. If the fear of danger wasn't there, Dr. Grinker concludes, they probably wouldn't have tried it.

The Wallendas are ambivalent on this. "Sometimes I get scared," says Tino, the twenty-two-year-old grandson, "especially in a new place. Say, if we've been working in front of five hundred people and then we do it for ten thousand, or we've been working at twenty feet and then we go to a new auditorium and start working at forty feet." Many apprentices have been taught by Karl to walk on a three-foot-high practice wire, he says, but then have gone up for their baptism at forty feet "and come right down and walked away." There was one, Karl remembers, who had been performing successfully for some time, but one night in Mexico City "something snapped" while he was halfway across the wire and they had to go out and rescue him. The man never walked the wire again.

Perhaps the most eloquent of the current Wallendas is twenty-year-old Delilah, a swivel-hipped brunette of remarkable poise and beauty who has "had the wire out there" in front of her ever since she was a toddler and who was spanked by her parents if, upon losing her balance on the low practice wire, she simply jumped to the ground instead of practicing to fall and grab the wire. "It's not fear of the wire," she says, "it's respect for it. A little tension—or fear, if you want to call it that—is good. One reason my grandfather never lets us use the net is because he says we would get careless if one was there and we knew if we fell we wouldn't get hurt. Sometimes I am more tense than at other times, like when we are in a new place or we are rusty, but it's always good to be a little tense, and if you know what you are doing, and pay attention, and respect the wire, and understand the danger, you will walk the wire." Will she continue to do it? "It is the only thing I know. I love the feeling of being up there where there is danger. I could never drive a station wagon to the PTA."

By noon, following a live television interview across the river in Davenport, Karl Wallenda had forgotten the conversation with the workman about the tragic Seven-Man Pyramid in Detroit and was in a chipper mood as he went for lunch across the street from the armory in Rock Island. Carrying a large brown envelope full of contracts to be signed for upcoming dates, he fidgeted on painful, bone-chipped heels injured recently when he lost his grip on the rope from the platform and had to jump the last fifteen feet to take his bows. "See if you can get her phone number," he said, and winked, nudging his partner and motioning to a lush nude painting on the wall. The hostess, who wouldn't recognize him later, to her embarrassment, finally gave him a booth in a dark corner of the restaurant.

"I tell you the truth, the only time I was ever really frightened was at Tallulah Gorge, in Georgia," he said in his heavy German accent as the waitress brought him the first of two martinis. Tallulah Gorge is a deep perilous canyon in the Southern Appalachians, and as a stunt to attract tourists to the area he was paid ten thousand dollars to walk across it on an eleven-hundred-foot cable some eight hundred feet above the rocky bottom. For three weeks, at a total cost of eighty thousand dollars, a crew of forty strung up the cable. A week before the event Karl and his wife, Helen, set up their house trailer at the site and Karl checked out things and gave out interviews to an international press corps."One woman called Helen and said she had just talked to God and God had told her Karl Wallenda was going to die. But those hypocrites don't bother me," he said. "What worried me was when this pilot told me the down drafts are so bad there that light planes are not permitted to fly near the canyon. I was thinking of that when I got on the wire the next day. The wind was very strong, and when I looked around I saw no helicopters. Now, I know how to fall off a wire and catch it. That is why I am never afraid. But I thought to myself, 'If I fall and catch the wire, who is going to come and get me?' So I watched the wire and I walked as fast as I could." He also did two headstands for the crowd of thirty-five thousand, rushed into the trailer, and downed the obligatory two martinis Helen had already mixed for him.

He is, as it turns out, totally pragmatic about the dangers involved. He never practices, he says ("At my age, why bother?"), and he is more comfortable walking the wire than flying in an airplane. "If something happens to the plane and I am sitting in the back of it and it starts to go down," he said, "there is nothing I can do. I am like this about automobiles. I want to drive it, not somebody else. I want to have control over a situation. If I die, I want it to be my fault." He is more nervous, in fact, when Delilah is on the wire. "If I am up there doing the tricks, it is all right. But when I am on the platform watching her I get pools of water in my hands.

I tell her, 'Delilah, be careful, my granddaughter,' and most of the time she laughs at me. She is a cold one."

"Could you teach me to walk the wire?" I asked him.

"Sure. I taught Luis in six weeks."

"But I've got acrophobia. Fear of heights."

"Have you played sports?"

"Baseball. A long time ago."

"Well," he said, "it doesn't matter either way. What matters is whether you *want* to walk the wire. No. What matters is whether you *need* to walk the wire. You must be a little afraid, and you must want to prove you are not afraid. Then. *Then* you can walk the wire."

Almost from the day he was born out of a suitcase in 1905, Karl Wallenda has had a need to perform. His parents, like their parents before them, had a small traveling outdoor vaudeville show in which the entire family was expected to participate. When Karl was five he was being hurled through the air by his parents, who specialized in trapeze, and by the time he was seven he was doing handstands atop church steeples to draw attention to the show when it hit new towns. "I had to do a lot of clowning, too, and I never liked that, because a clown had to be a dumb guy, and I never liked being a dumb guy." Karl attended some 160 different schools during those years, some of them for only a week, and at one point (when his father ran out on his mother) did handstands in taverns to bring in money for the family. "Even when I was able to go to school I would sit in class and draw sketches of the circus. Always I was dreaming of the circus."

His introduction to the high wire came when he was fifteen and, faced with another off-season working in the Alsace-Lorraine coal mines, read an ad in a newspaper for "a man that could do handstands for an aerial act." He took the train to Breslau and met a man who had put up a sixty-foot-high wire and was trying to start a sensational new stunt: The man would do a headstand on the wire, a woman would hang below the wire by her teeth, and another man—young Karl Wallenda, if he made it—would do a handstand on the man's feet. "I found out that fifty had quit before I got there. I thought, 'This man is crazy. I'm a guinea pig.' "

But he had no money to return home, so he lied about his age and worked on his handstands at night in a grim room and, three days later, won the job. "I just did it. It is that simple. I did it." It was the making of the Great Wallenda. A year later he was starting his own successful high-wire act at Berlin's Winter Garden, and in 1927, he accepted an offer to go to Cuba for a year. ("What could I do in the wintertime in Germany?")

It was in Cuba that the first Wallenda family was formed, with Karl and his wife and brother Hermann and a man named Joe Geiger. They were discovered by John Ringling. In April of 1928 they opened the Ringling Brothers Circus at Madison Square Garden to a capacity house, the four of them forming a three-level pyramid with the use of balancing poles and a chair, getting a fifteen-minute ovation. More than seventeen years later Karl was playing with the notion of the Seven-Man Pyramid when John Ringling died, and Ringling's successor, John North, "thought the idea was crazy and wasn't interested," according to Wallenda. Just after World War II Wallenda quit Ringling Brothers to start a renegade circus that lost a hundred thousand dollars in one year (at a time when he was methodically paying to get thirty-seven relatives and friends out of postwar Germany). He then went on his own, with his family act, where he has been ever since.

Today the Wallendas live in quite another world from that inhabited by most of the circus people who cluster around the shabby "winter quarters" on the edge of Sarasota. Karl and Helen Wallenda live in a tidy, two-story white frame house in a shaded neighborhood close to town and are constantly seen around Sarasota society. Karl is a four-times past president of Showfolks of Sarasota, the seven-hundred-member circus organization, and he averages one hundred pieces of mail each week. Every afternoon when he is at home the spacious side yard fills up with cars as friends drop by for a ritualistic three-thirty cocktail hour. An old-country burgher whose only hobbies are playing penny-ante poker with circus cronies and collecting spoons from around the world (he has a twelve-thousand-dollar collection of 740 of them and has willed the collection to the Circus Museum in Sarasota), he is your basic patriarch ("Karl is sometimes too kind and considerate to others for his own good," says a friend, explaining why Wallenda is not a rich man by any means). The only discordant note in the life of the Great Wallenda, in fact, seems to be found in the curious situation surrounding Mario, the adopted son, who was paralyzed at Detroit. Mario seldom comes around anymore, although there is a specially constructed ramp beside the Wallenda house for his wheelchair. "I have to read the papers to keep up with him," says Mario, with some sarcasm. Mario is now thirty-two, with a family of his own. "I don't regret what happened. Sure, I wish I could walk. But I knew what could happen. If you play with fire, you're gonna get burned. Everybody knows that except Karl. The thing is this: He doesn't care."

By nine o'clock at night, shortly before they would take to the wire for the first time in Rock Island, a tinge of anxiety noticeably visited Karl Wallenda and his two grandchildren and Luis Murillo. Karl had spent the afternoon doing more interviews and taking a short, fitful nap in his motel room. Delilah had worked four hours on the floor of the auditorium as a "computerized fortune-teller" at $1.65 an hour ("I can eat on this and put the rest in the bank"). Tino and Luis had double-checked the guy wires, to make certain they were still taut, before sleeping through the afternoon themselves. Now, dressed in their flashy sequined costumes sewn by Helen Wallenda, they nervously prowled about the cramped, cold dressing room beneath the stands while a pair of young men warmed up the crowd by doing acrobatics on a trampoline set on the stage beneath the wire.

"How is the crowd?" Wallenda asked the promoter, a friendly crippled fellow from St. Paul who had booked the Wallendas before.

"Not a thousand yet."

"First night's always bad."

"Yeah, and it's Ash Wednesday."

"Ash Wednesday?"

"Yeah. How am I supposed to know that?"

Wallenda took Delilah aside and told her about some changes. Tonight, for the first time, it would be she rather than Karl on the chair balanced on a rod held by Tino and Luis. "Just take it easy and don't be afraid," he told her. Staring aimlessly at the wall, she smiled faintly and said, mocking him, "Yes, Grandfather." Wallenda burst into a grin. "One time," he said. "If only one time she would admit to me that she is afraid."

And the show went on. Karl Wallenda walked across the wire, followed by the others, as the crowd hushed and the band played circus music. Then came Luis on a bicycle and Tino behind him and Karl with a headstand and Delilah with a handstand and Delilah on Tino's shoulders as he bicycled across. Gasps and applause came from the crowd, act after act, until finally the lights went down and the band built to the finale in this ratty little auditorium in the middle of America. Lights down, music up, for The Great Wallendas. Tino and Luis edged across the wire, a metal pole secured at each one's waist, with Delilah perched on a chair supported by the pole. Once they reached the center of the wire, they stopped. Karl stood on the platform and, with a bit of show biz, pretended to have sweaty palms and to implore them. "Careful, Delilah, careful," he said. There was a microphone strung around his neck. "Don't lean too far, darling. Not too far. Don't hurt yourself." They made it, to great applause. Five years later Karl Wallenda fell 120 feet to his death while trying to walk between two new hotels in San Juan.

Good Old Boys Never Die

Daytona Beach, Florida

God Bless America. It is Speed Week, which is the National Association for Stock Car Auto Racing's idea of the running of the bulls at Pamplona, and the good old boys have taken over Daytona Beach like a brigade of dogfaces turned loose in Paris for a weekend. I mean, NASCAR has upgraded its image a lot lately, but not *that* much. The townies and the teenyboppers and the maligned hippies down on Main Street can only stand back and marvel at the sons of Cheraw and Opp and Kannapolis and Jesup as they surge up and down Atlantic Avenue in their Easy Rider glasses and their nylon zipper jackets, arms hanging out of Dodge Chargers outfitted with racing tires. Wallace stickers, and fins on the back to keep them from going airborne. Good old boys setting up a cacophony of throbbing engines and Rebel yells and old-time wolf whistles, casing the joint on the morning of the day before the Daytona 500. Not that the Daytona Beach Chamber of Commerce doesn't want them there, mind you. Making up for last September's off-season business with a vengeance, the motels are charging up to fifty dollars a day, five-day minimum stay, and the bars are hanging out signs that say TIME FOR A PIT STOP, and in some places they've even doubled the price of a pack of Doublemint. Bell bottoms, bikinis, hot rods, and racing stripes are all thrown together for a weekend of racing and other diversions, but the single most dominant force in town is the good old boys. There are four of them in a room at the Daytona Inn this Saturday morning, drinking grapefruit juice and vodka and trying to win friends and influence people.

"Now, you gonna get us some extra sheets. Right?"

"*Oui.*"

"And keep the ice coming."

"*Oui, monsieur.*"

"Hey. Where you come from?"

"France."

"Hey, I heard 'bout them French gals. Huh? What time you get off, honey?"

"Next year."

All of which makes the contrast even greater in Suite 202 of the Hawaiian Inn, down on the south end of the beach, the Hawaiian Inn being one of those bamboo-and-colored-lights places done up in early Pago Pago and with a nightclub show headlining a hula dancer. Suite 202 has been occupied, for the past three weeks, by Lonnie LeeRoy Yarbrough, of Columbia, South Carolina, who used to be a good old boy himself. It has been no more than ten years since LeeRoy Yarbrough was having to tow his home-built stock car to towns like Waycross and Valdosta and Savannah on weekends, racing on small, ill-lighted dirt tracks for one-hundred-dollar first-place purses in those towns, having to tow the car back home after the race to cut down on expenses. The first time he raced at Daytona International Speedway, the NASCAR technical inspectors sent him back to his home in Jacksonville six times—LeeRoy pulling his car home in the middle of the night to work on it in his garage and then taking it back to Daytona for another inspection—before he finally satisfied them that he was safe enough to run with the big boys. But that was a long time ago. In 1969 LeeRoy Yarbrough won a record seven NASCAR superspeedway races, including the Daytona 500, and became stock-car racing's all-time one-season money winner by raking in some two hundred thousand dollars in purses alone. So, all of a sudden, on the eve of the 1970 Daytona championship, he finds

that he has orbited beyond the world of the good old boys whence
he sprang. It is mid-morning on the day before *the* NASCAR race of
the year, and he has nothing else to do but sit on the sunlit bal-
cony in a pair of checkered bell bottoms and a spread-collar shirt
and buckled pirate boots, reading about that afternoon's final
pre-500 race in the *Daytona Beach Morning Journal.* His wife, Gloria,
left for the beauty parlor at dawn, his six-man crew is crawling
over one of his three racing cars at the speedway; his business
manager and his financial adviser are taking care of things at
home; his white Mark III is glistening in the parking lot just below
where he sits; his private plane is tied down at the airport; and the
only thing to break his serenity is an occasional good old boy's
double-clutching a '63 Chevy as it roars past on the broad avenue.
LeeRoy gets a Seven-Up from the kitchen and then sits on a sofa
beneath a huge trophy he has picked up in a lark earlier in the
week.

"Yeah," he is saying, "I'm in the process of getting moved into
my new home, so I'm going back home right after the race. I gotta
mow grass and move furniture in and try to figure a place or a way
to get all my trophies in."

"What's that one behind you there?" he is asked.

"I was just fixing to tell you about that." He laughs and jiggles
the ice around in the glass. "They had this Subaru car down here,
this little bitty thing with about twenty-five horsepower, and
something sorta like a toboggan course to run 'em in. It's sorta like
running through heavy sand on a beach out there. Well, I got to
thinking about that thing and decided I was gonna try to win, and
son of a gun if I didn't. Won five hundred dollars, the trophy, and
a Subaru. Don't know what I'll do with the thing. Probably put it
in the trunk of my Mark III."

"Another trophy to find room for, too."

"Yeah. That, and more taxes to worry about."

"Better than no money at all."

"Guess I ought to look at it that way," he says.

If you know the South of pine woods and truck stops and courthouse squares, and remember when that land was dotted with
grimy, dangerous quarter-mile dirt stock-car tracks, and can still

conjure up the image of what it was like on Friday nights at those places, then it is incredible to note the evolution that has taken place in this sport over the past twenty, even ten, years. Stock-car racing was a phenomenon that sprang up out of the violent, lower-class white rural South in the late thirties, sprang up as naturally as weeds in June, a phenomenon that directly reflected the way of life of those who involved themselves in the new sport. In the beginning the heroes were local moonshine runners who cared less about the skimpy purses they won than about the sheer exhilaration of sliding a hot car around a dirt curve without checking to see if the Feds were on their tail. It was a passionate world of fistfighting and drinking and hell-for-leather driving, a celebration of life for people at an economic level at which there was and still is all too little to celebrate about. But as the sport spread it began to take on refinements. Crowds grew, meaning more money, meaning cleaner tracks, meaning faster speeds. It became possible for a full-time driver to make a living, and in 1948 it became necessary to organize NASCAR in order to regulate the tracks and the drivers and the cars and the rules. Then came the "superspeedways," which were a mile or longer and were paved and caused speeds to go well over one hundred miles per hour. Detroit jumped in next, sponsoring racing teams and building racing cars in the belief that stock-car racing would sell cars, which it did, and still does, to fans whose blood still runs hot enough to carry bumper stickers like CHEVY EATER and actually to brawl over the relative merits of, say, a Ford or a Chevrolet. Interest spread to other parts of the country, and tracks grew in New England, on the West Coast, and in all of the border states where Southerners had migrated for jobs and spread the gospel.

And so, today, stock-car racing has replaced baseball as the dominant grass-roots sport in America. It still thrives in some of the rural areas, of course, but it is primarily found at Daytona and at Darlington, South Carolina, and at Atlanta and Charlotte, on high-banked asphalt superspeedways accommodating crowds of more than fifty thousand. The races are generally won by "factory" drivers, former good old boys who are completely subsidized by Detroit manufacturers (even down to their tires and piston rings). Some fly their own planes and earn a hundred thousand dollars or more a year and have a crew to look after their winged machines and have their names on franchised businesses (fast foods, mobile homes, etc.). ABC-TV has signed a fat contract to televise some of the major races. Petty Engineering, of Randleman, North Carolina, has sixteen full-time employees to keep the cars of Richard Petty and Pete Hamilton ready to run all of the big ones, which just about squeezes the "independent" driver out of the big money. The new breed of stock-car-racing champion is faced with a whole set of new problems. This became most obvious when the king of the superspeedway tracks was built out in the wide-open spaces near Talladega, Alabama. The track cost six million dollars, has curves banked at 33 degrees, is a 2.6-mile trioval, and right off the bat the cars were hitting 220 miles per hour on what straightaway there is. But when the drivers began complaining of weird physical sensations after turning the track, medical tests were run, and it was found that they were suffering from the same problems that plagued the U.S. astronauts during *their* early training: problems such as vertigo, cyclic vibrations, and amplitude G forces. They were, in short, blacking out and getting bug-eyed when pulling 2½ G's on the high-banked curves. That is coming a long way from bucking a rattly jalopy around a flat dirt quarter-mile track.

LeeRoy Yarbrough is, in many ways, the symbol of this new breed of Southern stock-car-racing hero. He recalls with only a little nostalgia the way it used to be when he was hacking it out on the dirt-track circuit of the Georgia and South Carolina and north Florida swamplands, but he would be lying if he said he longed for the "good old days." He came out of all that, LeeRoy Yarbrough did, without getting killed and without having to give up the only thing he ever really wanted to do, and he has been able to adjust quite handsomely to the new world of racing stock cars. He is thirty-two now, a handsome man with moody, close-set eyes and thick dark hair (grown out, lately, in bushy, good-old-boy sideburns), heavyset but light on his feet. Although he has been trying to clean up his English, there is still the echo of dirt-track tire-kicking in his voice, and he never is quite able to pull it off when he tells important people he is "quite honored" with a new trophy and will "cherish it forever." Because he was known as a cocky hard charger with only one goal in life—winning—when he was a rookie, his recent attempts at public relations do not always pan out. ("Yeah," says a sportswriter who knew him when, "when he comes up grinning buddy-buddy at me I can't forget the times he was down and wouldn't give you the time of day.")

The plane, the new house, the Mark III, the mod clothes, and the financial investments (he says he is one of the major individual stockholders in Daytona International Speedway) are manifestations of his success as a driving champion, and someday soon he may quit driving to run a racing team of his own. But the major force in his life is the urge to slip behind the steering wheel of a very good car and see how fast he can make it go. He estimates that he does just that some two hundred days a year, whether it is running for first place in a race like the Daytona 500 or revving it up in a tire test at two hundred miles per hour over the Talladega track. When he races now, it is only over the major superspeedways ("I'll run about twenty-five Grand National races a year, maybe ten or fifteen others; I think we ought to let the Modified boys have their races to themselves"). He is backed by Ford Motor Company (although, the day after the Daytona 500, Ford announced it was pulling back on its participation in stock-car racing, meaning Yarbrough would have to start taking care of some bills himself), and this year he had three 1969 Ford Talladega machines. Three years ago he hooked up with Junior Johnson, the former NASCAR hero, when Johnson retired from driving, and Johnson heads the six-man team of mechanics who keep the sleek Yarbrough Number 98 blue-and-white Ford ready. Yarbrough entered his second Indianapolis 500 this year and expects to run more road races "and other type racing." When last year many of his fellow NASCAR drivers felt the Talladega track was unsafe and formed the Professional Drivers Association, Yarbrough was a charter member of the group ("I just felt like we ought to have something to say about what happens to us out there"). He is, in short, a leading member of the new crop of stock-car-racing heroes: out of the same soil that produced the early ones but caught in the rapid changes that have been taking place, and most willing to cash in on them. What that means is that he is thinking less about getting together with the other guys for a beer blast after next Friday night's race and more about what's in it for the PDA if a new television contract comes along for NASCAR.

Yarbrough's roots are fairly typical. He was born in 1938, to a Jacksonville grocer and his wife. No one in his family had ever raced cars, but LeeRoy got himself interested in automobiles early and built his first hot rod when he was twelve years old ("All the other kids would play baseball or hang around the drugstore after school, but I wanted to be around cars"). He had been driving a car for two years when he got his first driver's license, and even then his father had to sign for him because he was underage. He had dabbled in the usual high-school sports, but he says that nothing seriously challenged him, and he quit school when he was in the tenth grade so he could race cars. He won his first race at Jacksonville Speedway, which is one of a series of dirt tracks on a traditional Southern minor-league racing circuit, and for some five years he hacked out ten thousand dollars a year the hard way: working on his own car, paying for parts, towing the car from one dirt track to another, making it in races that paid ninety dollars to win ("I always ran a couple of races a week I knew I could win"), doing it by himself until he landed a sponsorship from a local automobile dealer. Gradually his situation improved. As a teenager he had worked part-time for a cam grinder in town to finance parts for his hot rods, but soon he had two cars and was driving full-time. Finally in 1961, he was in NASCAR and went to Daytona for the first time. That was the year he had to make the half-dozen trips back home to get his car up to par, but he finished a decent fifteenth and the next year won the $4800 first prize in the Sportsman race to put him on his way. He had done his apprenticeship, and he was ready to play with the biggies.

"I don't think I ever made up my mind, just like that, that I was going to race," he is saying now. "It just happened. I just had this burning desire to race cars, so to speak, and all of a sudden I was doing it. I can't remember not being around cars." To this day, racing is his only interest. "That's why I sorta pulled off on some of my business interests when I found out they might require me to be at a meeting on a certain day, and got myself some people to take care of that for me." His idea of a good time on an off day is to take his wife (they were childhood sweethearts in Jacksonville) to a movie, leaving young LeeRoy Glenn Yarbrough (the middle name is for the late star Glenn "Fireball" Roberts, LeeRoy's idol) with a babysitter. "I've never been an also-ran," he says. Somehow it does not sound immodest when he says it.

He *was* an also-ran at the 1970 Daytona 500, of course.

Number 98 had qualified third for the race, and it looked very good for a Yarbrough repeat this year, but there are so many little things that can go wrong when there are forty-odd cars going 150 miles per hour, neck and neck, that it is foolish to bet on a winner. As it turned out, it was a bad day for several of the hotter names in racing—former winner Richard Petty went out on the seventh lap, Cale Yarborough on the twenty-first, and Indy driver A. J. Foyt on the fifty-eighth—and LeeRoy, after running third through the first hundred miles, had to spend seven costly minutes in the pits at the seventy-five-lap mark while his crew feverishly replaced an ignition coil. As it developed, those seven minutes were the difference in Yarbrough's winning the $46,000 first-place money and having to settle for his ninth-place payoff of $2725. The late part of the race had the crowd of 103,000 on their feet— Daytona is an electric blur of Goodyear blimps overhead and swishing, sexy "Firestopper" girls and sunglasses and roaring engines and piercing yells—and they watched one of the most exciting finishes in years as veteran David Pearson was taken at the end by a New England college dropout named Peter Goodwill Hamilton, driving one of the cars operated by Petty Engineering.

When it was all over, Yarbrough showered and was back in the garage area in twenty minutes to make a last check with his crew. As he walked up to his car, his hair still slicked down from the shower, he was met by three men wearing identical pale-blue Goodyear nylon jackets. The men stood quietly and looked at the car, almost afraid to talk to LeeRoy. Finally one of them said, "Ignition, huh?"

"Yeah, the wire," said Yarbrough.

"How'd it happen?"

"Hell, you never know. Jarred loose is all."

Another said, "You going to Talladega Thursday?"

"Naw. You?"

"Yeah, I reckon I'll go on. You get there later?"

"Uh-huh. I gotta go home a few days."

And they just drifted away. LeeRoy got a better grip on the tan leather bag that held his racing suit, zipped up his blue nylon jacket, and lost himself in the crowd beyond the garage gate. While he was working his way toward Gloria, who was at some distant point in the infield, Pete Hamilton, the winner, was being interviewed over the PA system in Victory Lane, surrounded by Firestopper girls and photographers and members of the Petty Engineering team. Maybe, you had to think, maybe Peter Goodwill Hamilton represented still *another* new breed of stock-car champion. For Peter Hamilton has absolutely nothing in common with all of those good old boys who ran the dirt tracks and came up in the traditional way. Pete Hamilton was twenty-seven, from Dedham, Massachusetts, the somewhat errant son of a former Northeastern University president, a dropout from the University of Maine, a grinning, blond Yankee bachelor who gave up playing drums in a rock band when he got hooked on cars. "In ten or fifteen years," Hamilton told the crowd, "I think a degree in mechanical engineering will be a prerequisite for driving in races like the Five Hundred."

"The Big O" Hangs 'Em Up

Milwaukee

To those who remembered when he was still "the Big O," the night before had been tinged with more than a little sadness. "Due to an injury," the public-address announcer had said after the pregame introductions of the Milwaukee Bucks and the visiting Kansas City–Omaha Kings, "Oscar Robertson is not in uniform tonight." The usual capacity crowd of nearly eleven thousand at the Milwaukee Arena had not seemed to know whether to applaud the mention of his name or bemoan his absence. Impassively joining the pre-tip-off huddle at courtside, he had slapped Kareem Abdul-Jabbar on his bony rump before slipping into a chair at the end of the bench to watch his teammates toy with the undermanned Kings. His replacement, Lucius Allen, proceeded to score 13 points and pass off for 8 assists and hold little Nate Archibald to a season's low of 19 points. A rookie guard named Russ Lee, being groomed for the future, got in for 18 minutes and even put the crowd on its feet by stealing the ball and going in for a stuff shot. The Bucks were ahead by 34 points when coach Larry Costello called them off and sent in the subs, who held on to move Milwaukee 3½ games out front in their division of the National Basketball Association. Through it all, the greatest guard ever to play the game of basketball had sat glued to his chair like a kid forced to sit in the corner of the room: popping bubbles with his gum, shuffling his feet, trying to look interested. He has learned everything there is to know about basketball except how to watch it.

Now, at ten o'clock on a mid-January Saturday morning, Oscar Robertson was alone again. He was propped glumly on a table in the basement training room of the gymnasium at Concordia College, a bleak little school on the fringe of downtown Milwaukee, while the other Bucks plodded through an off-day workout on the floor above. When you are thirty-four and trying to play your thirteenth winter of NBA basketball, your body no longer jumps when you tell it to. He had pulled a hamstring at the beginning of a televised game against Los Angeles the week before, and it wasn't responding. As the sounds of thumping basketballs and squeaking sneakers and chirping whistles filtered down the stairwell, he padded across the cold concrete floor in his bare feet to get another heat pad and to shove another cassette into the stereo somebody had left on a table.

"Old Man Robertson," he grunted, smiling wanly and returning to the padded training table against the opposite wall.

"Those things must be painful," he was told.

"Hamstring? Better believe it. Worst thing you can get."

"How much longer?"

"Maybe Sunday night."

"No. How much longer will you play?"

Carefully wrapping the steaming pad around a chocolate thigh, he never looked up. "One more year after this one," he said. "I'd like to win another championship. I think we can do it, this year or next. Thing about that is, you never get enough championships. If we won next year, maybe I'd still be saying 'one more.' " An acne-faced Concordia player who was coming by the training room for his own Saturday-morning therapy stepped into the doorway and, upon looking up and seeing Robertson, blushed and started to back out of the room until Robertson spoke to him and asked him how things were going. "Just listening to a little music," Robertson added, putting the kid at ease and inspiring an exchange about the state of each other's health.

In a few minutes, weary of just sitting there letting the heat seep into his thigh, Robertson began to put everything away and get into his clothes. "If it was baseball," he said as he slipped on a pair of mod trousers, "I guess I could take some shortcuts and keep on playing. I've learned to make the most of those brief times when I can rest, like during time-outs and sometimes on offense. But you really can't take any shortcuts in basketball. If you do, they burn you up. And I'm not used to being burned." With that he trudged up the steps, moved through the bright, cold air, slid into a feisty bright-blue Porsche (with an Ohio license plate showing only the letter O), and roared off to the Arena for another half hour of treatment.

It became painfully obvious, as the 1972–73 NBA season warmed up and got serious, that we were seeing the last of what many have felt to be the greatest athlete ever to play the game of basketball. Oscar Robertson may have left his best stuff back in Cincinnati, where for ten years he averaged 29.3 points per game and made the All-Star team each season and moved so far ahead in the all-time-assists category that he may never be caught. When he was traded to Milwaukee in 1970 after a disagreement with coach Bob Cousy, he did what he was supposed to do—teamed with Abdul-Jabbar to give the young Bucks their first NBA championship, of the '70–'71 season—but he was, by then, going more on guile than on his once-awesome physical abilities.

That first season with the Bucks marked the first time he had ever averaged fewer than 24 points per game (he slipped to 19). Last year he averaged 17 points and easily led his club in assists, but the nagging infirmities of age set in and forced him to miss 18 games with a strange muscle problem in his stomach. Midway through the '72–'73 season, here he was: benched with a hamstring, averaging only 14.4 points per game, out of the NBA All-Star lineup after 12 consecutive appearances.

"He was never really that fast, anyway," said ex-teammate Jack Twyman in Oscar's defense, but everybody who saw him knew he had lost that important half step. "I know he's slower than he was at his peak," said Costello, hedging, "and for some reason I can't get him to shoot as much as he should. But there's no reason why he can't play one or two more years." When people talk about Robertson these days, they are likely to use the past tense in describing what a player he *once* was. "God," says a Chicago magazine editor, "why didn't he quit when they won the championship? I hate to see guys hang on like this."

Whenever Robertson does make the final decision to retire, it will mark the end for one of the most gifted natural athletes of all time in any sport. Most people would concede that the world's supreme athlete in any year, anywhere, is the Olympic decathlon winner. Stars in other sports can excel on the basis of one strength—a quarterback can be a superb passer; an outfielder can hit home runs; a golfer can putt—but to win the decathlon a man must be able to do it all. Still, after the decathlon champion, many in sports would name as the world's second-best athlete the man who can do it all in professional basketball: the guard who can shoot from inside and out, who can play 48 minutes if necessary, who can pass off and run the team's offense and play defense and even rebound.

Of all the men who have played guard in the NBA, Oscar Robertson is the one who stands out. "He is so great he scares me," Red Auerbach once said. In his prime there was no way to stop him from doing anything he wanted to do. In six different seasons he averaged better than 30 points per game. Twice he even led the Cincinnati Royals in rebounds. For his career he averaged an incredible 10 assists per game in spite of the points he scored himself. Hungry and instinctive and fluid and remarkably quick at six feet five and two hundred pounds, he was the consummate basketball player.

"You give him a twelve-foot shot, he'll work on you until he gets a ten-footer," Dick Barnett once said in jest and frustration. "Give him ten, he wants eight. Give him two feet, you know what he wants? A lay-up, baby." His nickname, "the Big O," was perfect.

It doesn't exactly fit any longer, of course, although fans everywhere—particularly in Milwaukee, where they will forever be grateful for that first championship he so strongly figured in—continue to cheer him and remember him. His mail still runs about two hundred pieces a week and is, according to Bucks publicist John Steinmiller, "of a broader scope, from more different places, than Kareem's." When he is well, he starts, and he can still pass off or go to the basket like a man possessed. But the end is near, and he knows it, and he is more or less playing it by ear. "You can't play this game at eighty percent, so I have to learn to live with the injuries until they heal," he says.

His three-year contract with the Bucks runs out at the end of the current season, and he will likely sign for one last year. Having slowly invested in rental property, in both Cincinnati and Milwaukee, and salted other money away in such things as mutual funds, he should be very well set for a second career. Whenever that comes, there will be no panic. He has financial security, is close to his wife and three young daughters, has no regrets whatsoever, doesn't intend to stay in basketball as a coach or anything else, and looks forward to furthering his interest in real estate when it is over. (He graduated sixteenth in his high-school class of 171 back in Indianapolis, "but that was a long time ago.")

"My wife hates this car." If Robertson has a plaything, a toy, it is his Porsche. It will accommodate 150 miles per hour on the speedometer, and he has to fold up gently to get behind the wheel, but he is not averse to careening about the streets of Milwaukee in it as though he were one of those quick little cyclonic winds off Lake Michigan. "Says I'm a kid when I get in this thing. She's probably right." He grinned with quiet satisfaction as he grabbed one gear after another and listened to the engine whine.

"You like Milwaukee?" he was asked.

"Oh, sure. You get used to *any* place after a while."

"But not like Cincinnati."

"What do you mean?"

"That's where everything happened for you."

He blinked his eyes, which are always popped open like those of a toad prowling for insects. "Everything, good and bad. The days in college, the days with the Royals. I guess everybody's like that. You remember the people you came up with. Those days when we were losing more than we were winning were some of the happiest days of my life. We knew we didn't have that great a team, but we pulled together."

"You care to talk about Cousy?"

"We were just different, that's all."

"I noticed you didn't speak last night."

"What could we say to each other? I don't know what happened between us. Maybe it was a personality thing. The man's known to have this ego problem. Whatever it was, I'll never forget what happened. Look," he said, stopping in front of my hotel, "I've got to run down to the Arena for about thirty minutes. I'll come back up and we'll talk, okay?" He was gone in a whiff, the Porsche whining over the icy streets of Milwaukee, a world away from the dirt-farm country of middle Tennessee whence he sprang.

Told in the 1970s, the story of Oscar Robertson sounds curiously old-fashioned—almost like a Horatio Alger tale. More and more of the "new" athletes are young men who seldom knew adversity—they were born well, never knew hunger, succeeded casually—but Oscar's is quite another story. He was born near a community called Ashland City, outside of Nashville, Tennessee, in a farming area where "everybody was an aunt or an uncle or a cousin." Most of the people were black sharecroppers, including Oscar's great-grandfather, who had been born a slave and at one time was proclaimed the oldest person in the United States, when he reached the age of 116.

When Oscar was four or five years old his parents decided to move the family to Indianapolis so they could find work. His father became a garbage collector, his mother a maid, and Oscar and his two older brothers—not particularly liking the idea of living in a crowded city housing project—continued to go back and spend summers with their grandparents at Ashland City.

"We were poor, very poor," he says, "but we didn't know it. The best times were when we went back to Tennessee in the summer. It was a good atmosphere for kids. The air was clean, and we'd get up early and work hard all day. It was good to get away from the city."

Although baseball was the bigger game with the kids in his area then, Oscar got hooked on basketball when he was seven or eight years old because it was "a poor kid's game" and because of his brothers. (The oldest brother, now a Converse salesman in Pennsylvania, became a member of one of the Harlem Globetrotters' units.) In retrospect, basketball might have kept him out of trouble. "I never got into trouble," he says, "but the potential was there. A lot of my old buddies went to jail and got messed up in murder and everything."

After he played in the local Police Athletic League, it was time to move into high school, and just as his parents were divorcing he came under the wing of an eighth-grade coach named Tom Sleet. "He was the first major influence in my life. He'd played for Butler University, and he did more for me than I'd ever be able to repay." Oscar enrolled in Crispus Attucks High in Indianapolis, an all-black school with "a lot of poor kids who'd grown up having to steal." Sleet was like a father to him, advising him and the others off the court as well as on, and Oscar was pointed in the right direction when he became eligible for varsity basketball.

He became a legend at Crispus Attucks. It was apparent that he had been born with the physique and the instincts for basketball, and once he had been drilled in fundamentals by varsity coach Ray Crowe, brother of baseball's George Crowe, there was going to be no stopping him. Crispus Attucks won consecutive state championships in 1955 and '56, going undefeated the latter year—the first time that had ever been done in the tough Indiana high-school circuit—and all the scouts wanted the star, this young black kid named Oscar Palmer Robertson, to go to their college on a scholarship.

He finally picked Cincinnati, because it was close enough to Indianapolis for him to visit home regularly and because he had heard bad things about the racial attitudes at other nearby schools such as Indiana and Purdue. Also, Cincinnati had a co-op program in which he could alternately work and attend classes. (Oscar would study for seven weeks; then for the next seven weeks he would work on calculators for $1.80 an hour at the Cincinnati Gas & Electricity Company.)

During the next four years of his life he was to learn more lessons off the court than on. This was in the late fifties, hot after the Supreme Court's ruling on segregation in schools, when black people still could not even get a drink of water in many places all over the country. Except during the famous annual Indiana-Kentucky High-School All-Star basketball game, Robertson had never played on a team with a white player, and now he was becoming the only black on what had previously been an all-white team at Cincinnati.

"I'll tell you the truth: In spite of that, I had never in my life thought about color until somebody mentioned it to me," he recalls. People began mentioning it regularly, and in nasty ways. He was called "porter" and "redcap" and "nigger" in North Carolina. In Cincinnati he chose to stay away from a local pool hall when he discerned he was the only black allowed in—and that only because he was a basketball star.

In Houston, one day during his junior year, he almost quit when the Shamrock-Hilton shut its doors to him and he had to stay alone at a nearby black university. "I was lying on my bunk out there at Texas Southern, wondering why it had to be me. I thought, 'This is the last time I want to hear anything about team unity. The college uses you, and then this happens.' The only reason I didn't quit was I knew the coach hadn't had anything to do with it. From then on they made sure a hotel would take me, too, before they booked us."

In the beginning Oscar Robertson had been a quiet, scared black kid almost pleading to be left alone so he could play basketball and get a college degree. Very quickly it became obvious that his talents on the court would not allow him to continue being a loner. The University of Cincinnati had not been particularly well known in the past, but with the arrival of Robertson it became a basketball powerhouse whose name was on people's lips everywhere. During his three-year varsity career Oscar was incredible as he led the Bearcats to 89 wins against only 9 losses. He averaged 33.8 points per game and set 14 NCAA records, of which the best known was an all-time scoring mark not broken until Pete Maravich came along. One night when he was a sophomore he scored 56 points in a tournament game at Madison Square Garden. He made All-America for three straight years and was named to the

U.S. Olympic squad in 1960. During those three seasons, home and away, more than 800,000 paying customers saw the Cincinnati Bearcats and their big star play basketball.

Nobody was more aware of the drawing power of "the Big O" than the Cincinnati Royals, who were being upstaged in their own backyard by a mere college team. During Robertson's senior year the struggling Royals of the NBA had drawn only 58,000 fans to 30 home games, whereas the Bearcats had packed the house every night. When the Royals managed to draft and sign Robertson, it might have meant saving the franchise.

In his highly successful first NBA season Robertson saw that the Royals nearly quadrupled their draw to 207,000. There followed those ten happy years for Robertson at Cincinnati, which abruptly ended when Bob Cousy—who until Robertson arrived was considered the finest guard in pro history—came in as coach and decided "the Big O" had to go.

Certainly there was a personality clash between the two—the feisty Cousy of the great ego countered by the quiet and popular, but aging, local hero—and it was only a matter of time before Robertson was sent packing to Milwaukee to team with Abdul-Jabbar and win a title. (When the Bucks did win the NBA championship the next year, the city council in Cincinnati drew up a resolution congratulating Oscar for his part in it.) The Royals, figuring it was the least they could do for the greatest player in the team's history, retired Robertson's jersey, Number 14.

Remarkably, almost suddenly, Oscar Robertson is no longer the pop-eyed young gunner but, instead, almost an elder statesman. He was quoted once during his college days as saying everybody in the world was "phony," but that sort of thing doesn't come out of his mouth anymore. About as close as he will come to a controversial statement is when he ventures the opinion that a man has to solve his own problems because "people, on the whole, will let you down."

Thirteen seasons in the NBA, seeing the places and meeting the people, has brought immense growth to him. He is always willing to meet with kids or with fan clubs. He is liked and respected by everyone on the club. He has opinions on most issues but doesn't go off spouting them unless he is asked. The only time he has ever been visibly involved in politics was when Robert Kennedy was campaigning for the presidential nomination (Oscar would have been in Los Angeles with Kennedy when he was shot but had to cancel at the last minute), which is not to say he doesn't have his own feelings about politics. There are those who feel his image has always been a bit "fuzzy," which is probably correct. If so, it may be the product of some instinct the Southern Negro of his generation is unable to shake. In short, when you have been a poor black kid from rural Tennessee, you speak only when spoken to.

A possible sign of what kind of man Oscar Robertson is came later in the day when, after thermal-wave treatments at the Arena, he came by the downtown Ramada Inn to chat for a while. There was only one other black family besides his living in their suburban Milwaukee community, he said, and even today that situation makes social contacts with neighbors tenuous.

"I didn't tell my wife about it," he was saying, "but not long ago they invited us to an open house. We'd been right there all that time, and finally they were inviting us to somebody's house. Well, the more I thought about it the more I got mad. I'm sure they'd had secret meetings when we were thinking about buying a house there, and probably 'allowed' us in because of my basketball. I knew all of that. Well, when the party came up I turned it down. Told 'em I was hurt or something. I'm just not a social bug, and I don't like to do things just for show or because it looks nice. I had to make up my mind whether it was a genuine invitation, and when I decided it wasn't I just didn't go."

It is this strong feeling for principle that guides the man in his dealings with others. For instance, a night earlier in the season when he was signing autographs for a mob of adoring kids (Oscar is very good with kids and doesn't mind staying all night to talk with them or sign programs for them): "This grown-up shoved through the crowd, knocking the kids out of the way, and said he wanted an autograph," Oscar recalled. "I asked him to wait, and he started cursing. 'Are you in that big a hurry?' I said. He said, 'Who the hell are you to tell me to wait?' I told him, 'I'm in a hurry and I'm sure these kids are in a hurry. If you don't like it, get the hell out.' That really burned me up. I mean, here was a grown man who should have known better than that."

In nearly everything he says he shows a maturing sense of place. He has not, for instance, jumped on the "Afro-culture" band-wagon—although he seems to respect Abdul-Jabbar's decision to adjust *his* life radically—for what are, to him, perfectly sensible reasons. "I had an argument with a friend not long ago about my ties and 'straight' clothes, about not wearing a dashiki and letting my hair grow out. I tried to explain to him that my background is European: you know, forks, formal settings, coats and ties. All of my rules for everyday life evolved from Europe, not Africa. Now, I don't think that makes me an 'Uncle Tom.' I'm happy I went to an all-black school and studied black history, and I was happy I got to go to Africa last year on a tour. But the point is, it's not where I feel my roots are."

For nearly two hours, his feet thrown up on a bed, he talked lei-surely about everything under the sun—Vietnam, black athletes, his future—as calm and introspective as he is in his approach to basketball. At times it became difficult to remember this was merely an athlete speaking.

On the United States' relations with other countries: "That book *The Ugly American* is still the truest thing written about our foreign policy. We never seem to think about helping a poor coun-try until it becomes a war threat. You watch: No black country will be helped by the United States until it becomes a threat. We still go into these poor little places and give them tractors when what they need and want is a water buffalo."

On Bob Cousy: "I never had any words with the man. Maybe he just couldn't bear to have me around. I remember one time he said I might be the best guard in the pros *since he retired.* Whatever his reasons were for letting me go, I think he was wrong, and I'll never forget it."

On black athletes: "Sports has done a lot for blacks in the last twenty years. Money gives a poor kid a way out, socially and oth-erwise. You can have a lot of culture if you've got some money, but culture to a poor man isn't a necessity. The trouble is, a lot of the black kids coming along now aren't hungry enough to pay the price anymore. They're more aware of what's going on, but they've had a taste of affluence."

On coaching: "I could never be a coach, because I don't have the patience. It takes a different kind of person to coach. I've never even considered it."

On the tour of Africa Kareem Abdul-Jabbar and he made last year: "Kareem and I were used when we went to Nigeria. The ambassador, through one of his officers, said he wanted us out of his house by a certain time because he was having some guest over. This was absurd; this was an insult. I mean, weren't we guests? Anyway, he wanted us to do something he had been unable to do, which was to speak to the local military leader. This guy wouldn't speak to the ambassador because of Biafra. I started talking with the military man and told him, 'If you want to leave, I don't blame you.' I'm not an ambassador or statesman, just an athlete. I thought it was crude what they did."

On instinct and learning in his style of baskeball: "The way I play, it looks like I'm not working at it. People have always said that. Well, even the so-called 'natural' has to work hard on certain things. I will say, though, that I had the fundamentals down when I came to pro ball. Once you get into pro ball, you don't have time to think, 'If this guy does this, I do that.' You do things instinctively. And I was able to play on instinct because of the fundamental training I got from Ray Crowe in high school."

And about the economy: "This is a war economy. It always has been. You wonder what's going to happen to the economy when the war ends. We may go bankrupt."

"What'd the trainer say about the leg?" he was asked after a while.

"It's still bad. I'll try tomorrow night."

"It must be frustrating, sitting and not playing."

"Well," he said, "it had to happen sooner or later." He had to go, he said. His daughters had been skiing, and he was supposed to pick them up and deliver them to the house in time for the family to sit down together for dinner.

On Sunday night, the following evening, the Chicago Bulls

came up the highway to play the Bucks at the Arena. This is a blood rivalry between two very physical teams, and the place filled up early. BULLS ARE FOR STOCKYARDS AND PASTURES said a banner being marched around the court by two fans. Once again came the announcement that Oscar Robertson would not be in uniform, due to injury. He had tested his leg early, before anyone else had arrived, and didn't feel it was time to go with it yet. From the beginning it was obvious the Bucks were going to need Oscar back soon, bad leg and failing reflexes and all, because they needed somebody like "the Big O" to calm them down.

Not looking like a world champion, Milwaukee went on to win, 100–95, with Abdul-Jabbar having another big night, scoring 35 points and pulling down 17 rebounds.

In the Bucks' dressing room afterward Larry Costello sat on a table in one room talking to overcoated sportswriters while happy players steamed under the showers in another end of the clubhouse. Lost in the swirl, Robertson quietly sat on a stool in one corner and combed his hair. If you didn't know he was thirty-four, you would swear he was a rookie. As he watched the others he occasionally grinned at their jokes and their cavorting, as though he were a kid getting his first chance to see real NBA stars at ease, up close.

"This is one thing I'll miss a little," he said.

"Dressing rooms?"

"You know. The guys. Winning. It's part of it."

"Will it be hard to give it up?"

"No," he said without emotion. He stuck the comb into his bag and zipped the bag shut, ready to leave the Arena. "I've done the best I could. I've accomplished everything I could have hoped for. I'll quit when it's time to quit, and I won't look back. It was fun while it lasted."

Perfectly at peace with himself and the world, "the Big O" stepped out into the cold concrete corridor, where he was mobbed by dozens of youngsters who remembered who he used to be.

The Old Grad

Auburn, Alabama

What they do, see, is take any Polish joke you ever heard and change it around so it reads, "Did you hear the one about the Auburn man who—?" Auburn, when I was there, was called Alabama Polytechnic Institute. It was the "cow college" of the state of Alabama. Graduates of the University of Alabama went on to become lawyers and novelists and doctors and governors and senators. Graduates of API—later renamed Auburn University and becoming, in spite of its latest penalty by the National Collegiate Athletic Association for buying football players, a respected place to go and learn words—became veterinarians and county agricultural agents and home nutritional experts and gym teachers.

So they tell these stories, these slanderous stories, and they never let you forget that you went to Auburn. "How do you tell a rich flamingo?" one of them goes. Answer: "The one with the ceramic statue of an Auburn man in the front yard." And a birth announcement from an Auburn couple is a letter of apology from the people who manufacture Trojan prophylactics. And an Auburn class ring is the pop top from a can of Pabst Blue Ribbon beer ("See," former Alabama quarterback Ken Stabler was quoted as saying, "it's even got a built-in nose picker"). And then there was the Auburn man who tried to pick up a woman in a bar and was told by her, apologetically, that she was a lesbian. "So," he said, undaunted, "how's tricks in Beirut?"

It isn't easy, being an Auburn man, and it is especially difficult when your football team has turned sorry. Auburn's Tigers (or Plainsmen or War Eagles or whatever it takes to hold your cover) were having an awful year. They were young and erratic—they would stomp Ole Miss and then turn around and lose to Florida State—and this was hard to take on Toomer's Corner in what is one of your basic small Southern college towns. Auburn is a town of some twenty thousand, slapped out there on the undulating farm-pond plains of east Alabama ("Auburn," they call it, from an Oliver Goldsmith poem, "Loveliest Village of the Plain") where there isn't much else for the natives to do except fish for bream and pray for rain and wait for the Alabama-Auburn game.

It is a drollery to say that football is taken seriously at places like Auburn. During the late fifties the school's athletic department was slapped with two years' probation by the NCAA. This was for allegedly buying things for a pair of twins from the Alabama mill town of Gadsden. This came on the heels of another probation for buying a handsome quarterback from Huntsville. The penalty meant that Auburn, although national champion in 1957, couldn't play in a bowl game or be on television or do anything else "American." The morning of the announcement of that second probation I was walking to my job as a hash slinger on campus when I looked up and saw the only sign of student protest in my four years in school. "Auburn," read a homemade sign stapled to a telephone pole, "gives the world 24 hours to get out of town." And I must add the story of the night one of our '57 national champions cleaned out a bar on the outskirts of town and was found sitting in the gravel, staring at a full moon and rubbing this half-pound diamond-studded ring, and was asked if he'd broken his hand or something. "Naw, I was just thinking," he said, "this is the first time I ever had a chance to hit anybody with my ring. And I bet that sumbitch *hurts.*"

〰〰〰〰

The college football season is over, except at Alabama and Ohio State and those other factories that always manage to buy a better class of fullback, and I regard the end with some sadness. I love college football. The pros play football better, draw more people, make more money, get more time on television, and attract a more sophisticated audience, of course, but there is a certain madness about the college game which makes it more appealing. My wife and I saw Auburn's first home game of this particular season, which Auburn lost to a little piss-ant college named Southern Mississippi, and what happened that day tells you all you have to know about college football. Just before the kickoff at Jordan-Hare Stadium (named after two former Auburn head football coaches) there appeared a middle-aged black couple wearing sweatshirts that read MY SON IS NO. 21. Number 21 for Auburn, now, was a freshman running back by the name of James Brooks; this was his first game, but everybody had heard about him, and he was hope for the future. His parents got as much applause, from where we were sitting, as he did. James Brooks, a smallish and what the sportswriters call "skittery" runner, whirls like a baby cyclone when given the ball. On that day James alternated between flying with the wind and fumbling punts. When he flew, the people in our crowd slapped the Brookses on their broad backs; when he dropped the ball and stood helplessly watching a Southern Mississippian fall on it, we commiserated with the family. There came a point when we, sitting around the Brooks parents, didn't give a good goddamn what the score was. We merely wanted them to give the ball to James, that black kid from Warner Robins, Georgia, so he could make his mama proud. Maybe the litle devil had wings under those shoulder pads.

And so, later in the season, we drove down the road to the Auburn-Georgia game with friends. We tailgated the fried chicken and potato salad and fried oysters and biscuits cooked the night before, walked to the quaint old stadium surrounded by hedges, sat beside the two-hundred-member Auburn band for three hours, got half drunk in the sun, lost ourselves getting back to Atlanta, piled into bed, and started thinking ahead to the last game of the season. None of the others, for an Auburn man, really counts. Okay, we lose to Southern Mississippi on a fluke. Georgia Tech, as usual, gets lucky. Can't hardly beat LSU on Saturday night in Baton Rouge. Etc., etc., etc. But now, friend, we got a serious matter on our hands. We got the Alabama-Auburn game. We got a civil war.

This war is fought at a grim coliseum called Legion Field in west Birmingham, amid housing projects and blue skies and foreboding smoke from the steel mills. When I used to go there as a kid I was a frightened trumpeter in the Woodlawn High School Band ("Largest High School Band in Alabama"), and there would be maybe twelve thousand in the thirty-four-thousand-seat stadium, and our Woodlawn Colonels were such tough street urchins that the referees would come into the dressing room and check the tapes to be sure nobody was carrying concealed weapons. But this new Legion Field is something else. Now it seats more than seventy thousand—at about ten dollars a head, and no telling how high the scalpers go—and it reaches to the sky. There is a sign hung on the face of the upper deck that says WELCOME TO BIRMINGHAM, FOOTBALL CAPITAL OF THE WORLD, and you had better believe it. On the Saturday after Thanksgiving each year these seventy-one thousand crazies show up with their pom-poms and their flasks and their Auburn or Alabama stocking caps at Legion Field. Bart Starr and Ken Stabler and Joe Namath and Pat Sullivan and Jimmy "Red" Phillips and scores of others who later made it big with the pros have played here in this game. I suspect that even Namath would tell you the high point in his career was the time he, as a senior at Alabama, played against Auburn at Legion Field. I doubt that there is another college game in America, beyond the Michigan–Ohio State game and maybe the Oklahoma–Texas game, that can compare with this one. What you have here is a total of nearly a hundred players, most of them from little Alabama towns like Albertville and Evergreen and Opp, trying to kick the living daylights out of one another so they can save face for another year. "Ain't no way I can go back home and face everybody if we don't win this one," the *Birmingham News* always quotes one of the kids as saying on the eve of the game.

They go back home, of course, to become used-car salesmen or insurance agents or county agronomists or small-town lawyers. Past glories. Remember the time old J. D. ran that punt back against Auburn? Hey, yeah, and 'member that interception last quarter against 'Bama? Damn, and that tackle Joe Bob put on ol' Musso in '64? Ah. The hopes and the fears and the juices and the angers. How they do keep us alive and, for better or for worse, kicking. We walked away from Legion Field after the game, through the smog and the traffic and the snarling and the rebel-yelling, and we saw what the policeman on duty would surely later call a "disturbance." Along Fifth Avenue North an Emergency Medical Service ambulance was wheeling up in front of a bleak frame house. A man was down in the yard. Half of the men crowded around wore little Alabama red-and-white beanies, and the other half wore orange-and-blue beanies representing Auburn. The man sprawled between the two frame shotgun houses wore orange and blue, and he was not happy about Alabama's having won, 48–21, and he had talked the red-and-white beanie into breaking his jaw.

Fi$hing for Catfi$h

Ahoskie, North Carolina

There is something in the old baseball scout re-
minding us of grandfatherly chats, squeaky slip-
pers, soft wine, and a knowledge gained only through experience.
They have been there in rickety, skeletal bleachers in small Iowa
towns and on grassy knolls at downtown St. Louis playgrounds,
witnessing it all—wild-swinging young brutes who would discover
the curveball in Class D the year after signing, burly Okies who
would turn out to be afraid to pitch in front of crowds; crew-cut
shortstops who would invest their eight-thousand-dollar bonus in
beer and pool and frowsy blondes in McAlester, Oklahoma—and
now the men who discovered stars and signed them up to play
professional baseball turn up, graying and sixtyish, wiser than the
rest of us. After the frantic years of squinting out into hard-baked,
skinned infields, abruptly having to adjust their eyes from deepest
center field to the stopwatch in their wrinkled hands, they come
down to wearing loose alpaca sweaters and lazily lipping slender
cigars and treading gentlemanly in broken-in Hush Puppies and
speaking warmly to the parents of the top prospect in town.

Such is George Pratt. It is turning dark on the day after
Christmas. Pratt, who got as high as Class AAA as a player and

has recently been put out to pasture as a "bird-dog" scout for the Pittsburgh Pirates due to heart trouble, is sitting in the lobby of the Tomahawk Motel in Ahoskie, mumbling soft exchanges with a stumpy, aggressive fellow named Dutch Overton, the assistant principal at Ahoskie High, in the barren, swampy stretches of far northeastern North Carolina. They are idly waiting for the Pirates' hierarchy to fly in the next morning and try to sign the best pitcher ever to have come out of this part of the country: Jim "Catfish" Hunter, a former high-school phenomenon who went on to establish himself as genuine Hall of Fame material with the Oakland A's. These days, after a petulant violation of his contract by A's owner Charles O. Finley, Hunter trucks into his Ahoskie lawyers' offices each morning in a gray, mud-spattered Ford pickup with a dog pen in the back. Then Hunter spits tobacco juice into a Styrofoam coffee cup while major-league owners and their accountants sit at the other end of a long walnut conference table in a back room, wearing elegant dark suits and rummaging through stacks of tax tables and such, earnestly competing to make him the highest-paid player in the history of baseball. This has been going on for about ten days now and should end in about a week, when all of the clubs not faint of heart have their cards on the table. It is not unlike the auctioning of a prize bull.

"Time flies, all right," Dutch Overton is saying. "It wasn't ten, maybe twelve years ago I was assistant baseball coach over at Hertford where Jim was playing. Most times I'd wind up umpiring our games behind the plate. They'd always say, 'No wonder Jimmy wins. He brings his own personal umpire.' "

"Competitive spirit played a part, too," says Pratt.

"Say y'all talk with 'em in the morning?"

"Us in the morning. Cincinnati in the afternoon."

"Jim's out hunting if I know him."

"I would imagine that's the case, Dutch."

Pratt is showing off his 1971 World Series ring to a motel guest when Overton asks who he thinks will eventually sign Hunter. "The Yankees," he says flatly. "Clyde Kluttz is their top scout, and he and Jim go hunting together all the time. Jim could make an awful lot of extra money in New York, too, and don't overlook that. And the Yankees can start winning pennants again if they get him. If I had to bet on it, I'd say the Yankees."

When it was announced at a frantic press conference on New Year's Eve of 1974 in New York that the Yankees had persuaded Jim Hunter to sign what was easily the most awesome contract in the history of major-league baseball—the five-year package came to an estimated $3.75 million, including salary and insurance and deferred bonuses—the whole story read like a novel. It involved a Southern country boy suddenly inspired to give it his best shot in the Big Apple, a club owner forced by the commissioner of baseball to stay out of the negotiations, a general manager putting the finishing touches on what could become another Yankee dynasty, a kindly veteran scout who got the job done through the back door with old-fashioned friendship and trust, a sleepy little tobacco and farming town abruptly basking in national prominence, a mercurial sports entrepreneur finally letting his arrogance and stubbornness get the best of him, a generous portion of vindictiveness from several sides, and, less pronounced, a general restlessness over the traditional notion that a player is a slave until proved otherwise. The cast:

• *James Augustus "Catfish" Hunter.* Born and reared on a farm near Hertford, some fifty miles from Ahoskie on Albemarle Sound, signed with the then–Kansas City Athletics for a $75,000 bonus in 1964 and is now, at twenty-eight, the premier pitcher in baseball. Because fishing is a passion, he was nicknamed "Catfish" by Finley as a gimmick. Has won 88 games and lost only 35 over the past four seasons, with a career earned-run average of 3.12 (and in 37 World Series innings is 4-0 and 2.19). A country-cool good old boy, devoted to his childhood sweetheart and two children, stays close to home. Salary with the A's in '74 was $100,000.

• *Charles O. Finley.* Controversial owner of the Oakland A's who is always in spotlight: for proposing orange baseballs; for designing garish, multicolored uniforms; for firing a second baseman who botched a couple of plays in a Series game; for trying to make pitcher Vida Blue change his first name to "True"; for cut-ting corners on accommodations and salaries in spite of three straight World Series clubs. When he delayed paying Hunter the remaining $50,000 on his '74 contract, Hunter was declared a free agent by an arbitration panel. After the Yankees signed Hunter, Finley paid the $50,000 and said he would take the matter to the Supreme Court.

• *The Yankees.* Having traded Bobby Murcer even-up to San Francisco for Bobby Bonds in a case of grand larceny at the trading block, the Yankees became a gathering storm in the American League, thanks in large part to the canny purchases and trades of president and general manager Gabe Paul. In the Hunter pursuit the Yankees were driven by revenge as well: toward Finley, for not releasing Dick Williams from a contract with the A's so he could manage the Yankees; toward commissioner Bowie Kuhn, for not helping them in the Williams tussle and for slapping a two-year suspension on club general partner George Steinbrenner for being indicted on charges of illegal political campaign contributions.

• *Clyde Kluttz.* Originally from the Ahoskie-Hertford area, Kluttz is the scout who first signed Hunter for the Athletics, a decade ago, and is now, at fifty-seven, the Yankees' superscout. A mediocre catcher for nine seasons with five big-league clubs, Kluttz's top yearly salary was $10,000 ("I deserved every penny of it"). Hunter says, "Clyde never lied to me. He's my friend. That's why I signed with the A's and that's why I signed with the Yankees."

• *The Bit Players.* There was pitcher Gaylord Perry, who came from nearby Williamston, trying to talk his old buddy into going with his Cleveland Indians. And the dean of major-league managers, saintly Walter Alston, of the Dodgers, who wanted Hunter badly enough to fly coast to coast for a chat. And Gene Autry, the old cowboy movie star and singer who now owns the California Angels, who stood on the streets of Ahoskie handing out autographed Christmas albums he had recorded. And A's manager Al Dark, who showed up with his wife one night at the Hunter spread, claiming he "just happened to be in the area" for some appearances. And Dick Williams, Hunter's friend and former A's manager, now managing the Angels, in Ahoskie also to do some ear-bending. And even attorney Dick Moss, of the Major League Baseball Players Association, instrumental in breaking Finley's hold on Hunter and, as a result—time will tell—possibly tearing a chink in the historical "reserve clause" binding a player to one club for life unless traded or sold.

Much of the story's charm lay, of course, in its setting. Hunter lives an hour away, on a 113-acre farm, but when it was determined that he was free to sign with any major-league club, Ahoskie was selected as the bargaining table, since that is where Hunter's lawyers work, out of a quaint, old two-story brick building on Main Street. The second-largest town in sparsely populated northeastern North Carolina, Ahoskie (pop. 5500) is a farmer's delight, with ten churches, a handful of family-style restaurants, an ample supply of feed-and-seed stores and tobacco warehouses, and a textile mill that employs nearly four hundred workers. Only twice in memory has the town attracted any sort of national attention: when Lady Bird Johnson made a train stop to promote her national beautification project (the train doesn't stop there anymore) and when the funeral was held for a native son killed while performing with the Air Force's acrobatic Blue Angels. It is baseball country, though. From the area over the years have come such major-league players as Tom Umphlett, Enos "Country" Slaughter, Stuart Martin, Jim and Gaylord Perry, and now Catfish Hunter.

It was in Hertford (pop. 2023), some fifty miles south of Norfolk, that Jim Hunter was born—the last of four sons—to a tenant farmer and two-dollar-a-day logger named Abbott Hunter. Life wasn't easy, but when the chores were done Jim found himself competing with his bigger brothers at whatever sport came to mind. He was growing up tough and big and strong—as a freshman at Perquimans High School in Hertford he stood six feet tall and weighed nearly 175 pounds—making him a prep star in football and baseball during his four years. ("He was just a big old country boy who liked it rough," recalls Bobby Carter, who coached Hunter at Perquimans High and now coaches at Roanoke Rapids, North Carolina.) Hunter was a linebacker and offensive end ("He could've probably been a pretty good football player at one of the smaller colleges"). But it was in baseball that he began to attract attention. Playing shortstop and batting cleanup when he wasn't pitching, Hunter would eventually pitch five no-hitters during his high-school career—one of them a perfect game, on the day following Easter Sunday of 1963—and bring the major-league scouts flocking to the porch of his father's farmhouse. This was in 1964, the last year of open bidding for young talent before the free-agent-draft era began, and one night in the living room of the Hunter house young Jim Hunter signed his bonus contract with the Kansas City Athletics and Clyde Kluttz.

Those were the days when bonus babies had to remain with the major-league club, rather than being farmed out for nursing in the minors, so Hunter spent the summer of his eighteenth year pitching batting practice and occasionally posing for gimmicky publicity pictures, sitting on the lap of fifty-nine-year-old pitcher Satchel Paige (another Finley stunt and possibly the beginning of Hunter's long dislike of Finley). During the 1965 and '66 seasons Hunter won only 17 games and lost 19. But he came forward as a genuine star in 1967, the A's last year in Kansas City before Finley moved the franchise to Oakland, when his earned-run average abruptly dipped to 2.80. In 1968 he became the first American Leaguer to pitch a regular-season perfect game in 46 years, and in 1971 he began a string of 20-game seasons that now stood at four straight. Last year, when he finished 25–12 with a 2.49 ERA, he won the Cy Young Award.

But there was bad blood brewing between Hunter and Finley. Who can figure Finley? He gave Hunter $75,000 to sign, $5,000 for pitching his perfect game, another big bonus for winning 21 games in 1971, an investment in 1972 that netted Hunter $15,000 after taxes, and once lent him $150,000 to buy nearly 500 acres adjoining his own 100 in Hertford. That loan from Finley came in 1970, and it was agreed orally that Hunter would pay back at least $20,000 at the end of each season, plus 6-percent interest, until it was all paid off.

"We never had anything down on paper," Hunter was saying

one day at Ahoskie during a lull in negotiations with the various clubs. "I appreciated the loan. I really wanted that land next to my place. I knew I could pay back the money every year, with the kind of money I was making with the A's. But we got into the season, down into August, and Finley started hounding me about the money. I said, 'But I'm supposed to pay you when the season's over,' and he said, 'I know, but I'm buying a hockey team and a basketball team and I need the money.' Well, the worst part was it seemed like he never called me about it except on days when I was going to pitch. I started eight games that August and didn't have a single win the whole month. I was worried. One time I asked him why he never called except when I was pitching, and he said he didn't know who was going to pitch then. That's bull. Charley Finley knows more about that ball club than the manager—whoever the manager might be in a given year."

That was the beginning of the end of their relationship. Hunter sold off most of the 500-odd acres he had bought with the loan, so he could pay back Finley at the end of the year. From that moment on he simply lay low and tried to forget about everything except getting batters out, which he was now doing masterfully. His tactic worked until he let Finley charm him into a two-year contract calling for $100,000 a year beginning with the 1974 season ("It was the fastest contract I ever signed; I don't know what got into me"), only to see lesser players take their dealings with Finley to arbitration and, in some cases, win more pay. When Finley piddled around about paying half of last year's salary to Hunter's agent in deferred payments, Hunter immediately pounced. This time he contacted Dick Moss, of the Players Association, got the matter before an arbitration board, and became an ex–Oakland A. "I felt like I'd just gotten out of prison," says Hunter, "even if I did regret how the other players might feel about my leaving the club." So A's slugger Reggie Jackson: "With Catfish we were world champions. Without him we have to struggle to win the division." With Finley pleading that he had never fully understood his obligations in the contract, and vowing there would be hell to pay for anyone who dared sign Hunter, the battle was engaged.

At eight-thirty in the morning, three days after Christmas, J. Carlton Cherry—a bulky, balding native who is senior partner of Cherry, Cherry and Flythe, Attorneys—was already in his office, cleaning out wastebaskets from the night before. Cherry and Jim Hunter have been associated since Hunter signed his first contract and "discovered a baseball player needs help on some things." For better than a week Cherry and his partners and a harried coterie of secretaries had presided over a small mob scene that took place each day, all day. Another delegation of major-league executives would arrive and, for an hour or more, retire to a small conference room with Cherry and Hunter to make its proposition.

Carlton Cherry is no small-town hayseed lawyer working from a squeaky swivel chair in front of Great-granddaddy's rolltop desk. Although this was easily the biggest project he had ever handled, he had methodically gone about his business—making discreet calls to baseball and sports-agentry people to get the feel of the new opportunities open to athletes and sitting down with Hunter to put down precisely what was most important to him and his family and, finally, declaring that the store was open for business—and he stood to make enough off the month's work he was putting in to allow two more generations of Cherrys the best North Carolina can offer. The Tigers, the Orioles, and the Cardinals never entered the bidding for Hunter, for lack of that kind of money and for fear of wrecking "team morale," but the twenty-one other clubs had been busily exerting every imaginable pressure. Some clubs sent in personal friends of Hunter's, as the Brewers did in dispatching Mike Hegan, an ex-A's teammate, to Ahoskie. Other clubs would undermine the Yankees and Mets by using Hunter's devotion to family ("God, Jim, your wife wouldn't even dare go to the grocery store in that jungle up there"). "We're looking for the overall picture," said Cherry. "The living conditions, whether the club is a contender; the ball park, whether it is a 'pitcher's park'; the money, of course, and the security. The total package. We've told every club it has an equal opportunity, even Oakland, and that we'll do no horse-trading and make no special deals with any club."

The Yankees were going after Catfish Hunter with the doggedness that Hunter himself shows when stalking a deer along a somber inlet on Albemarle Sound, and they intended to get him. Their nearness to a string of pennants was a driving force and a bargaining point. The magic of the Yankee name—the Yankees almost never lost when Jim Hunter was growing up—was another asset. And they knew that when it came down to the crunch, they had in their corner a fellow named Clyde Kluttz.

Clyde Franklin Kluttz was reared in the same part of America as Jim Hunter, knew the same baying of dogs and lapping of water and the loose feeling of hanging around the steps of a country store telling lies and enjoying the company of men in no hurry to do anything more than savor life. Ten years ago, scouring the Southeast for prospects in behalf of the Kansas City Athletics, he spent countless afternoons keeping watch over young Jimmy Hunter of Perquimans High, in Hertford, North Carolina, and countless evenings having supper with the possibility of his signing Hunter to an Athletics contract. He, like George Pratt, of the Pittsburgh Pirates, was that grandfatherly sort a farm family and a wide-eyed young prospect from the Southern outback could trust, and when Hunter's free agency was declared Kluttz knew what to do. He flew to Norfolk, rented a car, drove to Hertford, and checked in for an indefinite stay at a motel twelve miles from Hunter's home.

While the executives and scouts from the other clubs made their appointments through Carlton Cherry and flashed in on Lear jets for their stiff presentations to Cherry and Hunter, Kluttz sat in his motel room and read papers and watched daytime television. When the day began to close down he got into his car and drove over for a family visit with Hunter. *What about living around New York City?* Hunter would ask. *Look,* Kluttz would say, *I hated it, too, at first, but people are people. You've got good ones and you've got bad ones no matter whether it's Hertford or New York.* Hunter would say, *But San Diego says they'll pay me anything I want,* and Kluttz would ask how many players from provincial cities like San Diego ever made the Hall of Fame. It was a steady, logical, neighborly, sensible bombardment that Jim Hunter could not resist. *When you are talking about three million–plus, what's a few thousand?* The Yankees had the cash. The Yankees, with him as their ace pitcher, would be in the World Series. There would be all of the endorsements and other side money in New York, money generally unavailable if you play in San Diego or Kansas City or Texas. *If eight million people could manage to survive in New York then why couldn't Jim Hunter and his family?* Having the matter boiled down like that, tossing and turning over it in the shank of the night with his childhood girl friend at his side, Jim Hunter could make but one decision: the Yankees, the Big Apple.

There would be the logistics of finalizing the deal. The Yankees could save considerable money on taxes if the contract were signed during 1974. A press conference was called for New Year's Eve, at the Yankee offices in Flushing. An attorney for the Yankees named Ed Greenwald scribbled out the terms of the contract on ten pages of a yellow legal pad as he flew by private jet to North Carolina. Cherry and Hunter met the jet at a country airport, and the jet then flew on to New York with all three aboard. Limousines were waiting. The group went to the Yankees' offices, and then there was much merriment, with the press corps furiously recording the occasion. A fishing pole, bought in haste for $13.21 at a sporting-goods store that evening, was presented Hunter by an aide to Mayor Abe Beame. Clyde Kluttz was introduced and began to cry. Gabe Paul passed out a statement saying that George Steinbrenner had not been allowed to work actively in the negotiations but had told Paul, "Anytime you have an opportunity to buy the contract of a player for cash, I want you to go ahead whenever, in your judgment, it should be advantageous to the Yankees." At a bar along Third Avenue, celebrating New Year's Eve when he heard the news, a fellow said to a *Daily News* reporter, "What does this mean for the price of hotdogs, peanuts, and beer at the park?"

Yes. Precisely. And along that line, during the weeks following the signing of Catfish Hunter for more than $3 million to pitch baseballs, there were those columnists and commentators who would speak with outrage at the very notion that such amounts of money could fall into the hands of the few—be it Hunter, the president of General Motors, or Nelson Rockefeller—at a time in

American history when unemployment and inflation were coupling to make it difficult for millions of Americans to put bread on the table or gas in the car. "How can a nation be in dire financial straits and yet treat its linebackers and pitchers as if they were a great natural, irreplaceable resource like gold or oil?" wrote Jean Shepard in the *The New York Times.* In spite of the excitement the Hunter contract generated nationally, this aspect of the story was not entirely lost on the citizens of Ahoskie, North Carolina.

Joe Andrusia is not as articulate as, say, Jean Shepard. But during the two weeks of visitations by major-league executives and lawyers the imbalance of it all had been gnawing at him. Andrusia, fifty-nine, runs the barber shop in Ahoskie, directly across Main Street from the Cherry law offices, and had himself a ringside seat for the whole affair. Late one morning he sat in one of his barber chairs, wearing his white shirt and Hush Puppies, reading in the *Norfolk Virginian-Pilot* about the death of Jack Benny, listening to gospel music on the radio. It was nearly noon, and there had been only one customer so far. "Kids don't even get haircuts anymore," he said, "and the working folks have taken to letting the wife do the job with a pair of scissors to save money."

"Been quite a show around here," he was told.

"Lots of famous people dropping in, all right."

"You gotten any autographs?"

"Ah," Joe Andrusia said. "I wouldn't walk across the street to see Gene Autry. Him or any of the rest. All of those people wanting to give one man that kind of money. It's crazy. Crazy." Andrusia was bored. He folded the newspaper and walked to the plate-glass window and idly slapped his leg with the paper. "Why should I be so excited when this doesn't put money in my pocket? Hunter's not from here. All he spends around here is dimes for parking so he can get rich and spend the big money in New York." There was a swirl around the entrance to the building across the street as reporters and network-television crews pounced and bounded after the big-league executives as they walked briskly to their limousines. Andrusia shrugged and mounted the barber chair again. "Jack Benny," he said. "He had a test for cancer just a month ago, and they said it was all gone. He kept complaining, but the doctors said to quit worrying. Then, all of a sudden, he dies from cancer. You've got that kind of stuff going on, and people out of work and families starving and that Watergate mess, and now they're over there across the street trying to give some country boy four million dollars to throw baseballs. Crazy. Something's wrong somewhere."

Readin' and Writin'

~~~~~~

"Yeah, some of these guys say they write better when they're hungry. Lemme tell you something. When there's a kid with a distended belly crying in the next room and I'm trying to write some crap to buy some groceries, I find it sort of cramps my literary style."

Jimmy Breslin

All of this—giving up my life's dream of being a baseball player and then abruptly deciding to become a writer living in some hole somewhere—becomes a jumble. I remember, as we all do, some specific moments. My old man was home for the weekend, and he was what they call "tailgating it" without his trailer, and we rumbled over to this grim baseball park in the shadow of Stockham Valves and Fittings and I made two errors and struck out twice. After the game I slammed my glove down onto the wet grass and said, "That's it," and in the cab on the way back home he said, "A quitter, just a goddamn quitter," and that was that. My mama cried and begged me to go to college—she said, really meaning it, that she would see that I was the first in college from our family—and so I went to Auburn to study engineering because the only friends I knew had gone to Auburn to study engineering. Auburn University, at that time, was number one in college football and on official disaccreditation in engineering.

So there I was at Auburn, working for room and board wherever I could, and my mama gave me five dollars a week when she could find it. I promptly failed everything the Auburn Engineering Department had to offer and was making perfect grades in English under a kindly man named Walter D. Jones. I never knew that I knew the English language. I had never responded to tyrants. But Walter D. Jones was a gentle man who had spent his entire life nursing poets and assorted others of his ilk. He called me in one day toward the end of my first quarter at this strange, technically oriented college on the high farm-pond plains of east Alabama. This was in a musty old room in the mustiest old building of a college founded around the time of the Civil War, and here a dewy young student and a quiet-spoken gentleman professor sat talking. Echoes rang around the place.

"Paul," Walter D. Jones said, "you write very well. Clearly and to the point." I am sure there were coughs.

"Well," I said, "thank you very much."

"I'm sure," he said, "you undersell yourself."

"Sir?"

"You wanted to play baseball. You told me."

"Well, yessir. But I wasn't so good."

"Have you ever thought of journalism?" he said.

"Journalism. That's newspapers?"

"Journalism is newspapers."

Wanted: Riters

I f there is such a thing as a favorite suicide note, mine would be the one left by an author driven up the wall by the frustration of putting words together for a living. His name was W. J. Cash, whose *The Mind of the South* is still the classic tome on what it is like to be Southern, and this is the note he left before he did a one-and-a-half gainer out of a Mexico City hotel room: "I can't stand it anymore, and I don't even know what it is."

Writing is a mean and lonely business that pays very few of us for our time, but we tend to close our eyes to that part. I am entering my ninth year as a full-time free-lance writer, and I suppose I have done all right: three books, with two more on the way, and some 150 national-magazine articles. The life has been okay. It is better than when I worked on newspapers, where you learn to write. Newspapering was best characterized two decades ago by Paul Gallico. Gallico has written about his last day on the job, when he, one of the best-paid columnists in America, checked in one Sunday afternoon to write his Monday column for a New York paper. Waiting for him at the elevator was a greasy printer with a stubby cigar who said, "Well, Gallico, is that crap of yours going to be ready on time tonight?" Gallico wrote, in his column for the next day announcing his retirement, that that remark "sort of cramped my literary style."

Nearly everybody wants to write for a living, whether he be seven years old or seventy, and only God and Bennett Cerf would know how many unfinished novels lie a-molding in pantries across America. After all, didn't Grace Metalious write *Peyton Place* at the kitchen table? Maybe you can't take your royalties with you, but you can sure as hell leave your name registered with the Library of Congress. Nobody ever heard of a beautician or a truck driver or an accountant or a salesperson who could do that.

Predictably, this obsession has created an obscure but thriving industry in the country: the "how to write" business. Bookstores have a loyal market for such compendiums as *Writer's Guide.* Aspiring writers breathlessly await the monthly arrival of those magazines that tell how to write articles and how to sell them. A "famous New York publisher" travels the nation endlessly, holing up in hotel rooms as though he were a Hong Kong tailor, reading pitiful manuscripts and promising to have them published (at the author's considerable expense, and for a fee). Correspondence schools such as Famous Writers pretend to teach your local plumber how to produce a memorable novel. Many of these endeavors lean to the shabby side, preying on people misled into believing that anybody can write if he just has the time, but their profits more than offset their costs for legal counsel. And then you have the writers' conference, which is a different animal altogether.

A writers' conference is a gathering of hopefuls, usually in the summer at some semiexotic spot in the provinces like St. Simons Island or Marblehead, where everybody serenely writes and thinks and listens to alleged experts on the subject of writing. I never really believed in the effectiveness of such conferences, any more than I believe that great reporters necessarily come out of journalism schools, because I don't believe that writing is something that can be taught. "I went to college not to be taught how to write," says a Southern novelist named Harry Crews, "but to learn how to make a living while I taught myself to write." They nod knowingly when you tell them that, the students of writing classes and writer's conferences, but still they come.

I was prepared to be a bit smug, then, when I finally made one of those summer conferences as a guest lecturer. Working free-lance writers have little time or inclination to join societies of any sort, and most of my peers regard them as collections of little old ladies who present awards to one another. There were fifty stu-dents—from English teachers to grandmothers—and for a week they listened and wrote. Few showed talent, their manuscripts running toward religion and grandchildren and nostalgia and first-person articles for the "women's magazines," and I was tempted to tell them flatly to be realistic and give up the dream.

But I would never go back to one of those conferences and rec-ommend that they give up their dreams, any more than I would advise my son to give up baseball if he failed to make the all-star team, because I know the alternative. There is something wonder-fully innocent and passionate about the quiet fervor for words. Better they are there playing around with the language, however futilely, than staying at home watching television beneath an air conditioner. God knows the printed word is in enough trouble as it is without our running off the few who really care.

Okie

Among my friends is a fellow known as Streetcar, a name he was given when he was fourteen years old and he commandeered a trolley one shadowy Halloween night on the streets of Knoxville. Thus began a life of mischief for Streetcar—nothing really serious, just enough to get him into a startling succession of juvenile homes and county jails—which has continued, relatively unabated, for nearly three decades. He has hustled pool all over America. He has dealt in high-stakes poker games. He has awakened in bus stations in Arkansas when he was supposed to be in Miami. He has hung out with Hank Williams, claiming to have been present at the creation of several Williams songs. Unable to resist his charm, one Knoxville newspaper fired and rehired him as a sportswriter nine times. "Breathe deep, honey, and I'll pay the damages," he once said to a Playboy Bunny, just before setting her stockings ablaze with a Roi-Tan Blunt. It isn't that Streetcar is a bad man; he simply has his own private muse.

The last time I saw him was a couple of years ago. I was riding through Ohio on a magazine assignment with Merle Haggard. At the time, Streetcar was under the protective custody of his married sister in Columbus, a durable woman who played the organ in church and found ingenious places to hide her whiskey. Knowing he was terribly lonely, probably wasting away by eating Oreo cookies and watching daytime soap operas on television, I called him from Dayton and invited him to meet me at the Columbus auditorium when the Haggard entourage pulled in. The next day he bounded out of his sister's car at the appointed hour, sloshed through the puddled parking lot, and—looking like a drowned rat—proceeded to recapitulate old times and to make up for two years away from good Scotch.

While we were talking, Merle Haggard awakened from a nap in the rear of the bus and came up the aisle to the front. Waiting for him was a television producer in the midst of filming a documentary, an executive from the country radio station sponsoring the night's show, a *Life* photographer, and a local newspaper reporter. Through the windshield Haggard could see about a dozen fans already waiting in the rain to see him or touch him. Streetcar whispered to me that maybe he ought to get off the bus, with all these important people Haggard had to meet, but I told him to wait.

"Merle," I said, "I want you to meet Streetcar."

"What?" said Haggard, rubbing sleep from his eyes.

"I'd like you to meet an old buddy of mine."

"No, the name."

"Streetcar."

Suddenly Haggard's eyes lit up as they do when he hears a good lyric or finds an old fiddle. "How the hell did you ever get a name like that?"

And they were off and running for the next half hour, the new King of Country Music and this itinerant character from that American outback of pool halls and jails and bus stations. The TV man, the radio executive, the reporter, the photographer, and the adoring fans could wait. "Well, I'll tell you," Haggard was saying to Streetcar at one point, "nobody knows unless they've been there." They talked about places where they had done time, freights they had hopped, fights they had lost, women they had known. Much later that night, standing backstage as the show came to a close, Streetcar was uncommonly quiet. He listened intently to every word Haggard sang, and when it was over, the two of us standing outside in the cold drizzle, Streetcar looked up for the moon and said, "Hank Williams."

Success can be a hazardous business, no matter what your line of work, but it can be especially critical for someone involved in the arts. Money and fame have turned more heads of artists—writers, painters, poets, lyricists, performers—than any other outside forces. "Man was a good writer until he made some money," Ernest Hemingway once said of another novelist, failing to recognize that once *he* became rich and famous he spent the rest of his career parodying himself. Many a songwriter was at his peak when he was begging people to listen to his songs. Material success gets in the way of art, bleeding the juices and distracting the soul whence great art comes. It is a sad old story and can be witnessed almost daily in Hollywood and New York and Nashville: yesterday's starving prophet, today's well-fed hack.

Outwardly, Merle Haggard has changed considerably over the years since "Okie from Muskogee" won most of the big Country Music Association awards for him and made him a true superstar of American music. Now he demands upward of $10,000 per show, lives in a $250,000 home on a lake outside Bakersfield, California, fishes from a fully equipped yacht, and travels with two $100,000 buses (one for his band, the Strangers, the other for him, his wife, and his manager). He is playing all of the big places now, like Harrah's at Lake Tahoe, rather than the dinky nightclub circuit, and they want him for television and the movies. He can buy anything he wants, do whatever he wants to do, go wherever he wants to go. He has found the brass ring he was looking for during all those years of working the "fightin' and dancin' " clubs and playing country fairs and begging disc jockeys to play his records.

And, from what I see, an amazing thing has happened. Rather than spoiling the man, success has strengthened him. Five years ago he would come blowing into Nashville "to do some howling" and be seen stumbling around Music Row like a lost soul, but today he has all but quit drinking. In the past he was a moody man who seemed terribly complex and haunted by all sorts of devils, but now he is as self-composed as any man I have ever known in show business. The money and fame have worked for him, not against him, giving him a self-confidence and a freedom he had never known. Not having to worry about paying the bills or becoming a success or otherwise proving himself, he now has the peace of mind to go on and become what my friend Streetcar and a lot of other people think he can be: an artist whose work should be every bit as lasting as that of a very few, such as Hank Williams and Jimmie Rodgers. "I tell you what," Kris Kristofferson told me once, "that man has already written some of the best folk songs that's ever been done. I think that now, when we speak of Merle Haggard, we aren't talking about how he's going to come out on the Country Music Association Awards this year; we're talking about posterity."

It is really quite simple, to me, why Haggard did not have his head turned—did not sell his soul and his art—when success finally came. It is because he has remained true to his roots. He plans to die in Bakersfield, right there where his Okie parents migrated during the thirties. He would much rather be out fishing with some longtime crony than kowtowing around a network television executive on a golf course. His mother, who suffered during his boyhood days of wandering, still lives with Merle's family and is titular head of his fan club. His personal manager is an old boy named Fuzzy Owen—there is no telling how much money Haggard might be earning if he had a high-powered agent—but it was Fuzzy who virtually picked Merle up off the streets when he got out of prison, and Merle respects that obligation. It is not in his system to forget where he has been, and it is when he writes about those experiences—as in "Mama Tried" and "Branded Man"— that he is at his best.

Those experiences are something else. Merle was born in 1937, when the family was living among the sagebrush in a boxcar that had been converted by Mr. Haggard. The Haggards had bailed out of East Oklahoma along with many other burned-out farmers and rumbled up and over the Rockies to the Promised Land of California. Mr. Haggard was a hardworking, honest man who had given up the fiddle when his wife, a stern member of the Church of Christ, objected to such carrying-on. At the age of nine Merle had just begun to pay some attention to music when his father suddenly died. Mrs. Haggard felt perhaps too strongly her responsibility to raise her youngest son properly, and by the time Merle was fourteen he began skipping school and investigating the world on his own.

"It was the wrong thing to do," Mrs. Haggard says now of her decision to put Merle into a juvenile home for a few days to frighten him into straightening up. He promptly escaped, getting himself a record, and for the next ten years he was into everything: bogus checks, escape, burglary, petty theft, pitching hay, stolen checks, riding the rails. "Wild hair is all it was," he says. "You'd be surprised what a kid's thinking at that age. I mean, like the first time I got locked up I felt like I'd finally become a man. That's what it was all about. I was just trying to grow up."

If so, he did it the hard way. Late in 1957 Bakersfield authorities, tired of dealing with him, charged him with attempted burglary and escape and sent him off to San Quentin. He spent three years there (and was in the audience the day Johnny Cash came by to perform), straightened up when he spent a week in solitary confinement next to the doomed Caryl Chessman, and drifted back home to Bakersfield.

Off and on, between stretches in jail, Merle had got into music by writing an occasional song and picking guitar in roadhouses. When he returned from prison Bakersfield was beginning to sprout a modest music industry. Buck Owens and others had built studios, and plenty of clubs featured live country music. Soon Merle was quitting his job as a laborer and going into the clubs full-time. He met Fuzzy Owen, who eventually recorded Merle in a garage "studio" he had built. The first release sold two hundred copies, but not much later, in 1965, Merle did "All My Friends Are Gonna Be Strangers," and it made the country top ten. He signed with Capitol Records, rounded up a band, bought a station wagon, and hit the road. Within six years he had become a star, mainly on the strength of such autobiographical songs as "I'm a Lonesome Fugitive" and "Swinging Doors," which strongly identified him with working people and the downtrodden. Then, of course, came "Okie from Muskogee."

The story surrounding "Okie" oozes with irony. In the beginning the song was written on a lark. "We were riding through East Oklahoma and saw this sign that said 'Muskogee' and somebody said, 'I bet they don't smoke marijuana in Muskogee,' and somebody else threw in another line," Haggard recalls. "We must have pretty much written the song in twenty minutes." During the session when it was recorded, everybody kept breaking up over the lyrics ("I didn't think we would ever get it down," says one studio musician).

Before the record came out Haggard sprang the song on a beer-sodden crowd of Green Berets at Fort Bragg, North Carolina. He was astounded when they tore the place up. Then came the release of the record, and Haggard found himself in the middle of a controversy. In some quarters he was being hailed as a "proletarian poet" (President Nixon wrote to congratulate him on the song), but elsewhere he was being castigated for capitalizing on Middle America's distaste for the hippie life-style. Just as liberals had begun to worship and respect Haggard as a folk singer in the vein of Woody Guthrie, he had taken what they felt to be a cheap commercial shot.

I sense that Haggard is mildly embarrassed about having written "Okie" and "Fightin' Side of Me." A man who has no taste for politics (he seldom reads, can't vote, and turns down invitations to appear on behalf of candidates), he simply wrote a couple of songs that in one way backfired on him. No doubt about it, they made him a superstar, "Okie" becoming his first gold album. They thrust him into a prominence transcending the world of country music and brought him untold riches, but they also taught him a lesson. The charges that he had gone commercial got in his craw. Cash was just beginning to be accused of getting away from *his* roots, allowing noncountry acts on his television show, and Haggard didn't want that to happen to him. Many performers would have gone on to make a career of being a professional "patriot," but instead Merle next tried to do a song about an interracial love affair, which Capitol refused to record on the grounds that it would be bad for his image.

The uproar over those two songs was really only another stage in the slow but steady growth of Merle Haggard over the past decade. "I remember when he first came back to Bakersfield and began singing," says Bettie Azevedo, Merle's secretary. "Fuzzy had to show him how to stop twisting his mouth up so funny." Back then, everything he sang came out sounding like Lefty Frizzell, who is still a hero to him. He went through a long period then when he was terribly shaky in front of crowds, perhaps the most difficult problem he has had to overcome. Then he was leaning too heavily toward songs about boozing and unrequited love, which he began to break away from when he started going to his own background for material, with such numbers as "Hungry Eyes" and "Mama Tried." His marriage to singer Bonnie Owens was a stabilizer ("He's an Aries, very restless, and I have to remember that," Bonnie says), and his acceptance by "counterculture" types in spite of their dislike for "Fightin' Side" and "Okie" gave him the confidence he needed to branch out. His re-creations of the sounds of Bob Wills and of Jimmie Rodgers represent some of the purest country music I have ever heard (to be authentic, he taught himself to play the fiddle in six months for the Wills album).

What we have now is a man on the verge of becoming a complete musician, able to do it all—and in almost any medium. The catalogue of songs he has built up and continues to build runs the gamut—re-creations of greats like Rodgers, gospel songs, hard-beer-drinking classics, sweet love songs, even impersonations—and he may have already reached the point of being the most flexible country singer on the scene. "Let's face it, most of us aren't singers," Bill Anderson once told me, "we're stylists." Dave Dudley does truck-driving songs, Marty Robbins does gunfighter ballads, Cash does prisons and hard times. But Merle Haggard has run through them all and was last seen working on a Dixieland album. His one weakness, as I see it, is an inability to make his personality come across on television; he simply doesn't have the flair for show biz and hopping around that the screen calls for. There is a feeling around Nashville that Haggard will never achieve the spectacular success—financially, in particular—that Cash enjoys. A major reason for that, they say, is because he isn't good enough for TV and doesn't have the distinctive physical presence of Cash. Almost unspoken, though, is a deeper reasoning: that Haggard, unlike Cash, lacks the drive to go all the way. "I really think," admits Bettie Azevedo, "that Merle dreams of the day he can stay home to fish and write songs." It is frustrating for anyone, including executives who want to make a lot of money for Merle, to try to locate him when he is back home in Bakersfield. Capitol is forever having to reschedule recording sessions in Los Angeles when Merle doesn't show up. Merle even walked out on an Ed Sullivan Show, back when he really needed it, because they wouldn't let him sing what he wanted to sing, the way he wanted to sing it. He doesn't like to hang around with important people in show business, preferring to be alone, or with members of his band or with his family. He is, in short, his own man. Those very qualities that make him a beautiful man could be the same qualities keeping him from being a super-superstar.

The last time I saw Merle was during the past summer, when he was making a short swing through the South. He had played at George Jones and Tammy Wynette's outdoor place in Lakeland, Florida, rushed to Nashville for some recording, and had a date in Columbus, Georgia, before driving all night to Huntington, West Virginia, for another. At four o'clock in the afternoon Merle and Mel Tillis, who was also working the show, sat in Merle's bus outside the Columbus Coliseum, talking about songs and other writers and whatever.

"I thought you was gonna quit the road, Merle," Tillis was saying.

"I *was* getting pretty tired there," said Haggard.

"She's a booger, all right."

"Kinda got my second wind now, though. Got stale for a while, but then my tax bill came in."

"How's that?"

"Had to pay half a million to Uncle Sam for last year."

A young woman reporter from the local paper came by to interview Haggard ("I understand you write some of your own songs, Mr. Haggard"), followed by a couple of disc jockeys and then a pair of good old boys who wanted to audition a song for Merle right on the spot ("Tell you what, send me a tape so I can give it a fair shake"). He talked about the movie he may star in ("Sort of a *Grapes of Wrath* character"), played his latest record on the stereo, then reached for his fiddle and played a few strains from Bob Wills's "Faded Love." It occurred to me to ask him what he is shooting for, what he would like to be remembered as.

"I never thought about that," he said, squinting and looking absentmindedly out the window of the bus. The Coliseum was filling up very early, and it looked like a sellout. "A writer, I guess. Somebody who did some living and wrote songs about what he knew. Just like Jimmie and Hank did. That's all."

Quitting the Paper

Atlanta

On the *Kansas City Star* you were forced to learn to write a simple declarative sentence. This is useful to anyone. Newspaper work will not harm a young writer and will help him if he gets out of it in time.

Ernest Hemingway

L ate one night in the fall of 1969, with the rain splattering against the front window and the gray light of a television set dancing across the bar, I sat in a booth at Emile's French Café in downtown Atlanta with a feisty young newspaper reporter named Morris Shelton and methodically proceeded to get paralyzed on Beefeater martinis. By now this had become a daily ritual. I was thirty-three years old. I was the featured columnist for the *Atlanta Journal*, the largest daily newspaper between Miami and Washington. I had been one of a dozen journalists around the country to be selected to study at Harvard under a Nieman Fellowship the previous year. I fancied myself a sort of Jimmy Breslin of the South, cranking out daily one-thousand-word human dramas on everything from flophouse drunks to Lester Maddox, sufficiently loved and hated by enough people to have that sense of pop celebrity with which most newspapermen delude themselves. I had the most envied newspaper job in Atlanta, if not in the South, and now and then I would see a younger writer in a town like Greensboro or Savannah or Montgomery imitating my style just as I had once stolen from Hemingway and Breslin and too many others to talk about. I had been sloppy and inaccurate, from time to time, but I had also written some good stuff. I had hung around all-night eateries and gone to Vietnam and hitchhiked and lain around with hookers and shot pool with Minnesota Fats and sat in cool suburban dens with frustrated housewives.

And yet, with the next column due by dawn, I had run out of gas. I don't know why men make dramatic decisions at the age of thirty-three—change jobs, leave families, kill themselves—but they often do. "You have to remember," I recalled a friend's saying as he dumped a secure advertising job and ran off to Hollywood to write scripts, "we are no longer promising young men." I figured I had written a total of two and a half million words for five newspapers in the previous ten years, at a time when you had to move to another paper and another town for a ten-dollar-a-week raise, and about all I could show for it was bad credit and a drinking problem. Working for the mill, as it were, I was earning from Atlanta Newspapers Inc. a net of $157.03 a week; I was drinking too much, staying out all night, fighting with my wife, and choking on the notion that perhaps it was as a "well-read local columnist" that I had reached my artistic peak.

"No ideas for tomorrow?" Morris Shelton said, once we had run out of fanciful ways to cuss the paper. Morris was about ten years younger than I, an aggressive young Texan who hadn't yet chased enough ambulances and beat enough deadlines to be weary of it. He was one of the younger ones on the paper who defended me when the old-timers there called me a prima donna and, once I bailed out, much more vigorous stuff.

"Just a title," I said.

"You always start with the title?"

"This time I do."

"What?"

"Something like 'Quitting the Paper.' "

" 'Quitting'? You quitting?"

"You're my star witness, Morris."

And so we darted through the rain, up to the fourth floor of the old Atlanta Newspapers building, and while he dabbled around the newsroom I called my wife of the time to tell her the apocalypse had arrived ("Come on home and I'll have a whole bottle ready"). I turned to my typewriter and rattled a stark memo—"Dear Mac . . . I'm quitting newspapers because I am sick"—and then we went off to get supremely drunk at Manuel's Tavern. Manuel Maloof, counselor and padrone to scores of journalists over the years, was at first astounded and then fatherly . "You got a half-million people out there gonna be disappointed," he said. I said, "Let 'em all chip in a penny a week." When Shelton allowed as how maybe he ought to quit, too, I told him it wasn't his turn yet.

The next morning broke cold and bleak but, somehow, refreshing. There was the feeling that an exorcism had taken place; that I had successfully negotiated the move from one plateau of my life to another; that after ten years of writing magazine pieces and dabbling in nonfiction books, I would then move on to something else, like writing films or novels or both. I heard from Jack Tarver, of Atlanta Newspapers Inc., around ten o'clock, "astonished," wanting to know if there had been a personality clash—if so, he said, he could switch me over to the *Constitution*—but I told him the problem was bigger than that, and we quit as friends. By noon I had an agent in New York, by two o'clock I had a bank loan of $2,500, by five o'clock I had a modest office above a tire-recapping place, and by bedtime I had enough insurance—disability, hospitalization, life—to take care of a Marine platoon in combat. At some point during the day I drifted back to the paper to clean out my desk, while the old-timers glared tight-lipped at one with the audacity to quit ("Well," one was later quoted as saying, "it takes a certain breed of man to be a newspaperman"), and one of the young ones blurted that it "takes a lot of guts to quit like that." I said, "Christ, it takes a lot of guts to stay. I can steal the kind of money they're paying me." I thought, filled with myself, it was a Line to Remember Hemphill By.

Free-lancing isn't recommended for everybody, especially those with mortgages and kids and an attraction for whiskey ("Make your wife lock up the liquor cabinet and take the key to work with her" was the only advice I had for a friend who recently made the move). All of a sudden there is no Big Daddy to make you write, give you a paid vacation, pay your phone bill for business calls, make sure your typewriter is clean and working, let you take the day off, refund your business expenses, give you a Christmas bonus, deduct your taxes, cover your hospital bills, pay your post-age, clean the office, or pay you every Friday at noon. You are out there, alone, you against the editors and publishers in New York, and newspapers and advertising agencies all over the country are stocked with people who had once hankered for the day they could "get away and write." Making it as a free-lance writer requires many things—talent, energy, a financial cushion—but from my experience the most important quality is the motivation to go to the mines and write every day. It's a pisser. "I can't say I enjoy writing," somebody once said. "I much prefer having written." Your deadlines aren't at the copy desk anymore. They are at the bank.

Upon making the plunge, I was in better shape than some. My first book was making the rounds in New York, beginning to show promise—meaning they knew me up there and I could wheedle more advance money from my publisher. During the first week my agent got me a snap assignment for a sports piece, which quickly led to an association with *Sport* magazine. One piece led to another, and in spite of the shrinking magazine market I found I always had a half-dozen pieces to work on. My book got rave reviews, mostly, and it led to other books and other connections. I wrote for *Life* and *Cosmopolitan* and *Pageant* and *TV Guide* (I once considered printing up calling cards saying I would do "Anything legal or halfway moral"), and the business, as we say, expanded. There are the hairy moments when the checks are slow, and I have been locked in combat with my old nemeses Johnnie Walker, and the old debts from those years of wandering and grubbing along on newspaper pay make it necessary for me to produce better than two thousand dollars a month to stay out of jail. But it occurred to me when I was offered a fat chance to go back to newspaper columnizing, in a big Eastern city, that I am doing precisely what I want to do: writing what I want to write, when and where I want to write it, which ought to be about all a serious writer should expect out of his life. Now and then you have to write a little tripe to pay the insurance premiums (one more piece about country music or one more about minor-league baseball and they will have to come and get me), but it is the price you pay for relative freedom. Marshall Frady, an Atlanta writer who really does talk as expansively as he writes, said it one time in *Harper's:* "I think maybe writers ought to be scattered out over the land . . . [people who] just have this secret eccentricity to write. . . . And all the time, covertly, you're actually a kind of undercover agent stranded out in the cold, sending dispatches from the dark, brawling outback of life to Shakespeare, Cervantes, Dickens, all the others, letting them know what's going on now."

The temptation is to take out after the *Journal* and *Constitution* for their dedication to mediocrity over the years. God knows I've got a lot of good stories to tell. Atlanta and the South and the nation are teeming with talented ex–Atlanta newspapermen such as Jack Nelson, one of the country's most respected investigative reporters (now, alas, with the *Los Angeles Times*), who would have stayed on with the *Constitution* in 1964 if he had only been shown a single sign of love. Earning ten thousand a year at the time, Nelson told Tarver he would turn down the *Times* for something like twenty dollars a week and was accused of using the job offer as a "wedge to get more money." The paper made famous by Ralph McGill and his early-on pleas for racial moderation suddenly got a craw full of civil-rights coverage (i.e., "nigger news") and was one of the few of any size in America not to staff the Selma-to-Montgomery march. A star editorial-page columnist there was a retired Marine officer, John Crown, who addressed the Vietnam War with all the compassion and neutrality of a Holmes Alexander. The paper's best-loved columnist was old Hugh Park, waiting out retirement, who got a lot of laughs out of caricaturing the drunks and niggers and wife-beaters parading before Municipal Court every Monday morning. One of the most lyrical and sensitive writers they ever had was Harold Martin, but he was reduced to writing about squirrels and grandchildren before he quit in a huff when ANI wouldn't increase his pay from the twenty-five dollars per column he was getting twenty-five years ago. ("Consequently," he said, "I began writing columns worth twenty-five dollars.") And there was the night my first wife and I had to break away early from a Christmas bash at the home of my managing editor, Bill Fields, because I had to go and take phone calls until three A.M. on high-school football games so we could have some Christmas money. "Why, that's terrible," said the wife of the man who had made it all possible. "What a waste of talent." *Yes'm, that's what me and the little woman was thinking.* Bunch of dumb-asses. No wonder the newspaper business is in such a mess. They can't make up their minds whether they want unionized robots or writers. There have been a lot of good people with the Atlanta newspapers—McGill, Martin, Nelson, Eugene Patterson—and there are good ones now. But seldom have the good ones worked in management. There were too many times, in my day there, when the motto should have been (rather than "Covers Dixie Like the Dew") something like "No News Is Good News." If it cost money, or might cause legal trouble, it was likely not to be covered.

But all of that is another story, and from what I hear from others who learned to write on other newspapers, the *Atlanta Journal* isn't much different from the rest. A newspaper is (or was, before automation set in) a great place for a Linotype operator but a lousy place for a self-respecting writer to work. It is the first line of news gathering before the glamour boys move in for their glossy "in-depth" pieces and Dan Rather comes along flashing his teeth, and I have the greatest respect and gratitude for the grit and tenacity and dampered fury with which a great one like Jack Nelson firebombs the "public servants" hunkered down behind their stacks of press releases on Capitol Hill. But there aren't many Jack Nelsons. Most of us are inviting suicide or alcoholism or early senility if we continue to labor for too long at a newspaper, thinking we are going to uncover corruption and change the system, because most newspapers themselves are tidy, model plantations. "Boys," this beautiful old fellow on the *Constitution* copy desk would tell us summer interns as we waited for the last edition at one A.M., his voice broken from whiskey and his gnarled fingers yellow from cigarettes, "the newspaper is a monster. You fall in love with it, it's so big and strong, and you promise you're gonna feed it every day. But what you feed it is you. Every day you come in and feed it a little more, and then one day you're out of food. There's nothing left to feed the monster." I don't know whether he did it for emphasis, but he always then broke into a terrible coughing spell that was enough to scare the living hell out of a twenty-year-old journalism major.

What you do, then, is use the paper before it uses you—take what it has to offer about the craft of writing, which is almost everything—and then, as Hemingway learned, "get out in time." I am convinced that the newspaper is the writer's boot camp. You learn how to use the language. You learn how to interview people. You learn how to work under pressure. You refine what Hemingway once called a writer's "built-in shit-detector." You see things few others see, every day, for as long as you work at it. Unlike magazine writing, with its long time lag, you get an instant reaction to everything you write. But all of these are the fundamentals of good writing, and sooner or later many of us become restless with the discovery that there are the facts and then there is the truth. There isn't time or space or enough perspective to rush the truth into a newspaper. And so you either stay with the paper and go crazy with that knowledge or you simply thank the paper for its help and move on to places where there is more time to do the job properly. It seems to be an altogether natural progression.

The first full-time boss I had in the newspaper business was Benny Marshall. Benny had grown up in the country outside of Birmingham in Alabama. He attended little Howard College and, during the 1950s, became sports editor and sports columnist for the *Birmingham News*. A witty gnome who could cry at the sight of a wino passed out in an alley, and then make you cry when he wrote about it, Benny was a one-man show when I joined him as a writer of high-school sports in 1958: absolutely committed to reading, writing, editing, and planning the sports section. He would be in the office making up the paper at six o'clock in the morning, up in the composing room to oversee the makeup, back down to remake the home edition, out to Alabama football practice seventy miles away in Tuscaloosa, and back at his typewriter turning out his daily column as the sun went down. He was like a father to me. He boosted my ego and covered up my mistakes and gently showed me the way.

Benny was too good for the *Birmingham News* or any other newspaper. He was built more along the lines of a novelist, or at least a shimmering magazine writer; instead it was his lot to write two-column forty-two-point Bodoni Bold headlines and interview football players and fight cold wars with fat-bellied compositors. He never said it to me, but I suspect that a sense of dread began to fall over him around the early 1960s, when he turned forty and I left the *News* to wander. A terrible gambler, drinker, and womanizer—as prolific at each as he was at writing beautiful prose—he was strapped with debts and family obligations and a deteriorating body at a time when, perhaps, if he had gone on to the books and other things, he might have been doing great work. This was not the only cause of Benny Marshall's demise, but it certainly contributed.

One day in the fall of 1969, just before I was to quit the *Atlanta Journal,* I went through Birmingham on a column-writing expedition through the South. I hadn't seen Benny in some time, although I had heard from him now and then ("Fan letter," he scribbled on the envelope of a note to me in Vietnam, and "To One Who Passed This Way But Wouldn't Stop" on the flyleaf of a paperback collection of his columns), and I was irked when they said he was in New York accepting some kind of an award. I was sitting at his typewriter, rushing to finish a column on Birmingham before Western Union closed and I would have to drive on down the road to Montgomery, when someone answered a phone and turned to me. "You may have a chance to help out an old friend," I was told. Benny was at the airport, drunk, insisting on coming to the office. Maybe I could take him out for coffee in order to get him out of there. Thirty minutes later the elevator doors opened, and there he was, reeling drunk, waving a cup of coffee at me. "Hemp," he said, and we embraced.

Suddenly the executive editor of the *News,* Vincent Townsend, glowered from across the newsroom. Townsend was very good at glowering. He also had a son who floundered through more than one college, flunked the *Birmingham News* aptitude test, stumbled as a reporter, and finally, as part of his education before ascending to upper management, was put in charge of the paper's weekly pick-the-winner football contest. (Of course, Vincent Townsend intended to see that the football contest succeeded.)

"*Mister Mar*shall," Townsend boomed.

Benny weaved and spread his hands. "Chief," he said.

"Have you ever been to Siluria, Mr. Marshall?"

"Shiluria. Sure I been to Shiluria."

"How would you like to go back to Siluria?"

"Well, sir, I don't like Shiluria very much."

A fellow who ran a service station down the road in Siluria had won the week's football contest, and Townsend wanted Benny and a photographer to drive down that afternoon for a picture and a story. One of the others talked Townsend out of it, saying Benny was tired from his trip and that he would do it instead, and tried to straighten Benny up before driving him home. "You want to go in and watch a real ass-chewing?" Benny said to him. He stumbled out of the car, negotiated the walk to his front door, went straight to the bathroom, shut the door, put a .38 to his head, and pulled the trigger. The *News,* under Vincent Townsend's orders, said fine things about Benny in a front-page editorial the next day. I quit newspapering five weeks later.

Saturday

San Francisco

The typewriter was his escape. It was what kept him sane. It was portable, baby blue, with big, pica type, and he had kept it on the kitchen table since the day it had come in the mail with a letter explaining that he had won it by placing third in a jingles-writing contest. During the time he got the typewriter he had written several pieces—an essay about ecology for the *Atlantic Monthly,* a story about a hooker for *Playboy,* a profile of Charlie Finley for *Sports Illustrated*—but hadn't sold any of them. Last Saturday afternoon, at his apartment near Golden Gate Park, he was cleaning the keys when the phone rang. Becky, his wife, answered.

"Hello?" Becky said into the phone.

"Who is it now?" Ernie whispered.

"It's her," Becky said, cupping her hand over the receiver.

"Jesus."

"Two weeks?" The rent was late again, and Becky was faking it with the landlady. "Goodness. I guess we just forgot. Yes, ma'am. Well, it's Saturday, you know? I know it. How about if Ernie brings it by Monday? We were just getting ready to go out of town. Yes, ma'am, I know. Monday's all right, though. All right. Yes, ma'am."

Saturdays are never any good for Ernie. Other men take off for the golf course or go sailing or sit in front of the color television to watch football, but it hasn't been like that for Ernie in a long time. He wondered how long it had been since he'd played golf on a Saturday. Since the Saturday before he'd married Becky, he guessed. Before, when he was in college and his parents were coming across with spending money, there had been plenty of time to enjoy life. He was majoring in journalism then. He was going to run off somewhere and write novels. But then he met and married Becky. He dropped out of school and took a job in a department store, and the children began to come.

Now he finds himself trapped. He puts in eight hours every day, loading furniture into a truck, and every week he gets a check for $123.72 once everything is deducted. The rent comes to $175 each month. With three children it gets tough making the bills. He wants to be a writer—"I've got this great idea for a play about a guy who was an All-American football player and then turned gay"—but when he gets home to the apartment at the end of the day he is wiped out and Becky needs help with the kids and he winds up flopping out on the sofa and going to sleep. "Whatever happened to the old matron of the arts?" he was saying. "I need me a rich old lady to stake me while I write great things."

So Ernie's week has settled into a stultifying pattern of loading heavy things every weekday, falling asleep on the sofa every night, not writing anything of consequence, and drifting down the street to Sammy's bar on the weekend. Sammy has been impressed with Ernie ever since Ernie showed him the item he sold to *Reader's Digest* for the "Humor in Uniform" department five years ago. Sammy began to look at Ernie as some sort of hero when he saw the yellowed clipping with Ernie's name and address affixed to it. Ernie didn't mention to Sammy that it was the only thing he has ever sold from all of those hours at his baby-blue typewriter.

After the phone call from the landlady he went on down the street to Sammy's. Becky insisted on it. She even gave him a couple of dollars for some beer. That worried him, but he didn't know what else to do. He took a seat at the bar so he could watch the football game on the color television set hanging on the wall.

"Been writing any?" he was asked.

"Some," he said. "The novel."

"How's it going?"

"Slow. Slow as hell."

"What's it about?"

"The novel? Oh, about a young guy all messed up. Autobiographical stuff. Like most first novels. I'm thinking about ending it with the kid going in and telling his foreman where to get off."

"Happy endings are big."

"Yeah," he said. "A happy ending. Big stuff."

The phone rang in the bar, and Sammy said it was for Ernie. He walked around the bar and talked for a minute and then came back to his bar stool to finish his beer. "Becky," he said. "Goddamn landlady called back and said she wants the rent today. Two weeks late. I don't guess I can blame her."

Ernie left the bar and went to the apartment. He made a big show out of tussling with his two young sons and kidding around with Becky. Then he went into the kitchen and snapped the case on his typewriter and quickly walked it out of the house. Because he had kept it clean and in working order he got thirty-five dollars for it at a pawnshop in the Tenderloin. O. Henry would have been proud.

Ex Drops In

San Francisco

It is probable that Frederick Exley was the best-known unknown novelist working in America during the seventies. Ever since the publication in the late sixties of *A Fan's Notes* he has symbolized the enigmatic position of the serious writer in this country. That book and the publication of the second volume in an autobiographical trilogy, *Pages from a Cold Island,* did little more than further Exley's history of living on the economic edge. People in America don't want to read about poverty and alcoholism and suicide and divorce, which is what Exley writes about. They want to read Jackie Susann paperbacks about Hollywood and cocaine and boys doing erotic things with other boys. The best-sellers these days are not written by writers. They are written by shrinks and jocks and sex doctors and escape artists and gangsters and former White House people and other actors.

This is a hell of a time for writers. Billy Faulkner wouldn't be able to buy the groceries these days unless he found a way for the postmistress in Oxford, Mississippi, to get raped at high noon down at the railroad depot. You have to have sex or white-collar crime or an international conspiracy or UFOs or sharks to make it now. John Steinbeck published *The Grapes of Wrath* forty years ago. It was all about the rich versus the hungry. That, incidentally, is the test of a great novel: Can you sum it up in one sentence, or, better yet, one phrase? They called Steinbeck a communist when the novel came out in 1939 and it was 1962 when he finally won the Nobel Prize in spite of the flak. Good timing, there, John. Today nobody wants to read that crap. Reality, thy name is mud.

Fred Exley is pushing fifty years of age now. His life, once a disaster, is coming back together. He was born and reared in Watertown, New York, where his father was the all-time local football hero. That is what *A Fan's Notes* is all about: how the son of the small-time biggie manages not to cope. Ex went through divorce and whiskey and impotence and insanity—he doesn't bother to change his own name in the "novel"—but now he is making it. He paid his dues. Now he turns out to be something of a pussycat, living four blocks away from his mother in an apartment in Alexandria Bay, New York, where he cooks and cleans and washes for himself and drops into a neighborhood bar to drink with the same guys he once got into trouble with as a kid. "You Southerners like to talk about roots, like you invented it," he was saying the other day, "but I got news for *y'all*. Everybody wants to go back home."

His books are classics read mainly by critics and other writers and people eager to honor distinguished writers. The last he heard, *A Fan's Notes* had sold fewer than eighty-five hundred copies in hardcover (the author sees approximately one dollar per book on a hardcover) and was going into its sixth futile paperback attempt. *Pages from a Cold Island,* which came out in the late seventies, hasn't done a bit better. The final autobiographical work of the trilogy—this Exley journey through America—is called *Last Notes from Home,* and there is little hope that it will do anything at the box office. "What you've got to do," I was telling him yesterday , "is take up with somebody who can handle all of that money from your estate. Writers like you get rich fifty years after they die."

Ex just left. He spent two nights sleeping on our sofa—all right, one night, taking out for the evening he spent alley-catting—en route to Hawaii. He planned to spend six months or so at Lanai City—on a plantation, with somebody he went to kindergarten with—and to try to finish the third novel. Then he would go back home to upstate New York to do whatever was necessary for survival. A movie was made of *A Fan's Notes*—so bad that it never got below Canada—and there are always pieces to be written for the magazines.

Exley, having lived through personal disasters before, has more or less made a separate peace with the world. He is a novelist in the purest sense. He suffers and takes notes and lives to get even with the bastards. He is good and he knows it. He doesn't cotton to the literati hanging out every night at Elaine's in Manhattan and the Lion's Head in Greenwich Village and those pubs on Long Island like Bobby Vann's. He prefers to live near his mother and the guys he grew up with, up there in an isolated part of the country where it gets deep in snow about this time of year ("Going to Hawaii is a cop-out, like running from a fight, but it's *my* cop-out"), and to continue writing about what he has seen and lived through.

So. Ex and I had some fun together. My wife and I threw a party on his first night in town—all writers and editors, although the only guest who had read *A Fan's Notes* was a slump-shouldered socialist who once knew Bob Dylan in Minnesota—and Ex lay about the next night because of what transpired earlier that day. I was then the hot new columnist for the *San Francisco Examiner* and had finally been invited to one of the semifamous Round Table Luncheon gatherings thrown by an upwardly mobile divorcee named—for the present—Pat Montandon. Pat and her rich husband of the moment invite a dozen or so "famous" and "exciting" people, known as "personalities," to their elegant penthouse atop Nob Hill. Everybody sits around sipping cocktails and being served lunch by a German husband-and-wife team and then discusses important issues like Transcendental Meditation. The luncheons become Radical Chic pretty quickly. Ex and I, at any rate, warmed up at my place with bloody marys and then took a cab. "You want to frisk me?" Ex said to the guard at the elevator. "All I got is a flask." We ascended to the penthouse, had some martinis, and then everybody sat around the famous round table. Pat Montandon, as is the custom, went counterclockwise around the table.

Each person was introduced and asked to talk about what he or she was "involved with." There was Jessica Mitford and the founder of the National Organization of Women and an effeminate liberal clergyman and a token black and I, the displaced Southern son of a truck driver, and many others. Ex, this crazed novelist, was ordering more martinis and was wondering how far he would fall if he took a leap through the plate-glass window onto Jones Street.

"Frederick," Pat Montandon said when it came his turn, "would you tell us about yourself and what you are working on?"

There was terror in Exley's face as he wobbled to his feet, drink in hand, and addressed the assembly. He whispered to the German *Hausfrau* to sweeten his drink. There was a wheeze and a long pause. "My name," he told them, "is Fred Ex. I am an alcoholic." Then he sat down, and Pat Montandon issued orders to serve lunch immediately.

 War

"War orphans? Last week there were these three kids standing on a bridge and the first thing I thought was 'How come they ain't in school.' And the next thing I know is one of 'em is pulling a grenade out of his pajamas and blowing up Lieutenant Jones. This war is crazy. All wars are crazy."

Sgt. Gerald Houts, U.S. Army, Saigon, 1966

*L*ate in the fall of 1965 Lyndon Johnson and his administration decided to go whole hog after the war that
was going on in Southeast Asia. All of a sudden the number of kids from
America who were being sent over there, halfway around the world, to fight a
war hardly anybody but the Vietnamese understood grew from maybe 15,000
to 180,000. I wanted to go over there and see what the hell was going on.
The Atlanta Journal *finally* sent me for two months, during the spring and
summer of 1966, and I can recall only in the shank of night that once I was
there. I remember having a kid die in my arms in a bomb crater that spring,
and I remember bedding a sorry little girl, about sixteen years old, named
Desirée. I remember almost getting arrested by the Vietcong at two o'clock in
the morning at a place where I, in my Atlanta Braves baseball cap, wasn't
supposed to be, and I remember meeting bodies at airports and attending military funerals and talking to widows. None of it made any sense. When I returned to my paper in Atlanta I was asked by my balding ex-Marine managing editor when I had changed my stance on Vietnam from Hawk to Dove.
"Since the day," I told him, "that kid died in my lap."

It has been pointed out that these pieces, set against all the rest, are not
written in the first person. I write personally. But there is no way to write
personally about war, because war is murder. War starts out as a small ven-
detta between countries, and then the politicians come into it and all of a

sudden you have thousands of kids—the kids are always the ones who get it—shuffling through jungles and having their legs cut off and their wives leave them, and then the politicians make a "political issue" out of it. Meanwhile, of course, the politicians' kids are tucked away in college.

    War is unspeakable. You can't even talk about it. It is crazy and unending. One of the columns I wrote when I got back was about a kid who'd had both legs blown off by a Claymore mine in Vietnam. He was in the Veterans Hospital in Atlanta. My title for the column was "The Leavings of War." My editors changed it to something like "Sergeant Smith Recovers." When I complained, I was told by my ex-Marine managing editor that the Atlanta Journal *"is a conservative paper."*

The Telegram

Atlanta

T he cab driver did not want to knock on that door any more than Becky Sanchez wanted him to. She was asleep in the front room with David, the two-year-old, and it was a few minutes past six o'clock in the morning. It had been difficult enough for her to sleep lately, because the new baby is due any day and she has diabetes and David has chicken pox. They sleep on the same bed—a narrow little Army cot in the front room of the tar-papered frame house she and her two sons and her mother share with another family in the old part of Atlanta—and having her husband gone has not made it any easier.

It was still dark outside when the cab rolled down the bumpy street and stopped in front of 656 Grady Place SW. The driver looked at the telegram again, shivered against the cold, and walked up the steps and knocked on the door.

Becky Sanchez tried to clear her head. *Who in the world?* She slipped into a robe. She got out of the bed very quietly so she would not disturb David. She walked past the chest of drawers. On top of it were the tinted picture of her husband in uniform and the black Bible with the name "Frankie Sanchez" engraved in gold, the Bible the church had given him before he left. She found the doorknob. She twisted it and opened the door a crack.

"Are you Mrs. Rebecca Sanchez?"

"I'm she."

"I have a telegram for you."

"Who—?"

"Will you sign here, please?"

"It's so dark I can't see. Where?"

"Right here."

Becky Sanchez found the line on the form and initialed the telegram. Maybe it's Frank's mother. Maybe they're coming to visit. The cab driver said, "Do you have someone here with you?"

"Why, yes, my mother's here. And my boys. Why?"

"We're supposed to ask."

Becky Sanchez still didn't know what was going on. Without thinking, she shut the door in the driver's face. She walked around the bed where David was sleeping. She sat down on the edge of the bed. She tore open the yellow envelope and opened the telegram. There were two pages to it, and they had been stapled together. At the top of the telegram it said in capital letters DO NOT PHONE AND DO NOT DELIVER BETWEEN 10 P.M. AND 6 A.M. Then Becky Sanchez read the rest.

THE SECRETARY OF THE ARMY HAS ASKED ME TO EXPRESS HIS DEEP REGRET THAT YOUR HUSBAND, SPECIALIST FRANKIE SANCHEZ, DIED IN VIETNAM ON 23 FEBRUARY 1966 AS A RESULT OF GUNSHOT WOUND TO THE HEAD WHILE ON A COMBAT OPERATION WHEN HIT BY HOSTILE SMALL ARMS FIRE . . . PLEASE ACCEPT MY DEEPEST SYMPATHY . . .

Becky Sanchez blinked her eyes. *I must be dreaming.* She got up off the cot and walked across the cold board floor. The cab driver was still waiting on the porch. He did not want to look at Becky Sanchez.

"It's my husband," she told him.

"Yes'm. I figured that."

"He's dead. They killed him in Vietnam."

"Yes'm. Is there anything I can do?"

She said, "Can you take me to my preacher's house?"

"Yes'm."

Becky Sanchez stumbled back to the bed. She quickly wrapped David in a blanket. Tommy was sleeping in the other room with her mother. He would be all right. Becky picked up David and walked to the cab with the driver. They stopped at a neighbor's house to leave David, and then they went to her preacher's. Rev. Garland Odom, of Grace Baptist Church, wasn't at home. He was in south Georgia at a revival. When Mrs. Odom opened the door it was Becky Sanchez, wearing a robe and crying, and the two women embraced without having to speak. The cab driver was relieved to know he had done what they had told him to do. He fired up his cab and got the hell out of there.

Frankie Sanchez was born and reared in Dodge City, Kansas. His father worked on the railroad, and his grandparents had come into the wheat country from Mexico. When Frankie finished high school he worked for a while on a construction gang around home, and then, when he was nineteen, he decided to make a career out of the Army. He went to boot camp and then was sent to Fort Benning, Georgia, and that is where he met Rebecca Charlotte Morgan one day when she was visiting Columbus.

They married. Becky learned what it is to be an Army wife. Frankie had to leave her once to do a tour in Europe. Two sons were born. They lived in a house trailer. They hit all the Army posts, but they always seemed to come back to Benning, and that is where they were stationed last August when Spec. 4 Frankie Sanchez of the First Air Cavalry Division got his orders to go to Vietnam. Becky was expecting a baby. They prayed it would be a girl. Because most of the Benning doctors had also gone to Vietnam, she decided to move to Atlanta so her mother could help her through the pregnancy.

Army wives know what war is all about. They live with it in boot camp and they live with it at the washeteria and they live with it at night when their men are gone and there is nothing to do at two o'clock in the morning except look at the ceiling and imagine headlines about Vietnam. But they are never prepared for the cold consequences. They are never prepared for a telegram that arrives at six o'clock in the morning to tell them that the father of their children is dead.

The afternoon of the day Becky Sanchez got her telegram she sat on the edge of the Army cot in the front room of her dismal house. She wore a light-blue denim maternity dress and brown loafers. Her dark-brown hair was sweaty and awry. David sat on her lap eating a Fudgesicle. Tommy was down the street somewhere playing with his pals. The tinted picture of her hsuband, and the engraved black Bible, were still on top of the chest of drawers. The telegram lay with them. In the middle of the room was the white cradle filled with white sheets and fluffy blankets still in their cellophane wrappers.

"He was going to reenlist this June," she was saying. "I think, from his letters, he might have had a few doubts about staying in the Army since he got over there. But he's an Army man. He would've stayed in. When he left I just knew he was coming back. I never thought any other way. We didn't ever really discuss the war. He felt it was his duty to go, and that was that."

"When's the baby due?" she was asked.

"The doctors have said March ninth all along—that's a week from today—but I've got diabetes, and it made my blood pressure go up. I wanted them to induce labor, but the baby's not ready yet."

"The boys. How've they taken it?"

"They don't understand yet."

"Your last letter? From Frankie."

"A week ago. The day he was killed. I'll get it."

Becky Sanchez returned in a minute and opened the letter. David had sneaked out the back door to play in the dirt. "I won't read it all, because some of it's personal. But he said he'd been out for twenty-three days and had about two more weeks to go before he'd get three days off. He said in all that time they hadn't made contact with the Vietcong but once." She read from the letter: " 'Write and tell Mom I'll write her when I get more paper as this has gotten wet and it's all I've got. . . . Send me some dried fruit and last, but not least, a little girl. . . .' " He had bought a doll and some Vietnamese pajamas for it. " 'If it's a boy, it's gonna be the biggest sissy in the world. I won't be coming home until June or July so send me pictures of you and the kids. And if it's a girl I want you to name her Karen Dianne. . . .' " Becky Sanchez began to break as she read the end of the letter. " 'Tell the boys I'll be home before they know it.' "

After she had wiped her eyes and put the letter and the telegram away, Becky Sanchez walked out onto the front porch. David was playing with rocks in the front yard. The sun was slipping away. "I don't want to question it," she said. "I have my faith. I know it's the will of the Lord, but it still hasn't hit home. It's robbing him, not getting to see the baby, but I know he was saved before he left. If he had been lost, it would have been worse. He's in heaven now. That's better than where we are." She snapped at her youngest son. "David, you come on in the house, now."

Welcome Home,
Billy Goad

Atlanta

I t was five-ten in the morning, and there was a bright full moon overseeing the dark and the freezing cold on the ground. The wind whistled and groaned against the hangars and the baggage carts and the people and the parked planes, swirling and nipping at everything like a wounded and angry shark. Delta flight 892, a nonstop jet from San Francisco to Atlanta, was ahead of schedule, as usual. There were few people waiting to meet the plane at this time of day. The ground crew was already in place at Gate 45, waiting for her to turn the corner.

Charles Riggins stood beside the forklift, hunching over in his parka and hood, and tried to beat off the cold. "You got an HR on this one?" somebody said. HR stands for "human remains."

"Yeah," Riggins shouted.

"You get many of 'em?"

"From Vietnam?"

"Right."

He said, "About one a day. Maybe more. I don't know."

"You handled any personally?"

"Seven or eight, I guess."

"They hard to handle?"

"Naw. Forklift makes it easy."

The huge swept-wing bird was moving into place now. The revolving red light on her top threw red blips on the terminal. The ramp agent stood atop the generator next to the gate, his legs spread for balance, the wind flapping his trousers. She kept coming, rolling slowly toward the gate, whining like a tired horse. Then she stopped. The cabin lights were up. Sleepy passengers began filing down the aisle. The ground crew swarmed all over her.

Riggins mounted his forklift while they opened the small cargo hatch in the rear belly of the plane; then he raised the lift and inched it toward the hatch. Three crewmen rode the forklift and crawled off it into the hatch. You could see the crate in the dim overhead light. It was a rectangular pine box, battleship gray, with one brass handle on each end and two on each side. Stenciled on one end was the name SSGT GOAD, BILLY E. A white card said HEAD—KEEP THIS END HIGH.

The military escort, a husky sergeant with ribbons all over his chest and a black mourning band around his left sleeve, had come up now. He stood next to the forklift. His name tag said he was Staff Sgt. Charles A. Cameron of the Sixth U.S. Army Escort Unit. He watched as they struggled with the crate.

"Easy does it," one of the ground crew said.

"That back end, the feet, it goes first," said Sergeant Cameron.

"Hey, how about lowering the lift."

"That got it?"

"Naw. Lower your end so it'll move on the casters."

"Be sure it doesn't roll back on you," the ramp agent said.

"Okay. I got it."

"All right. It's clear. Let it down easy."

Sergeant Cameron jerked to attention as they eased the crate onto the forklift. He snapped a salute and held it until the crate was secure on the lift. Then he relaxed and bent over to help them spread a yellow slicker over the crate.

When the slicker was secure Sergeant Cameron raised up and said, "Where's the hearse?"

"Other side of the terminal," an agent told him.

"Very good."

"We've got a Jeep here for you."

"No, sir, I stay with the remains all the way."

"Okay, but it's plenty cold."

"It's my duty, sir. I'll ride the forklift." Sergeant Cameron swung onto the lift. Riggins turned on the lights. They eased away from the plane and headed across the stark runway for the transport terminal where a hearse was waiting to take the casket to Columbus, Georgia. When they reached the hearse they quickly loaded the crate into the back. Sergeant Cameron saluted again. Then they closed the double doors. Cameron's hands were splotched with marks from the cold. He was invited into an operations office for a cup of coffee before they drove on to Columbus.

One of the worst jobs they can give a military man is escorting what they call HRs. Your job is to see that everything is handled properly. Then comes the hard part: meeting the family and trying to make it as easy as possible to kiss off a life. Some of the family members are sick at the sight of a uniform, and they take it out on the escort officer. But you have to stick it out for as long as the family wants you around. That is your job, and when you have come back from a burial in Georgia you head out for Nebraska or Illinois or Utah. It is not a nice way to make a living.

Sgt. Charles Cameron is a good soldier. He has been in the Army for twenty-five years. He fought in Europe during World War II and was in Korea. He is due to retire in one more year but says he won't if the war in Vietnam is still on ("The Army's been my life and I can't desert it when it needs me"). He looks as a sergeant is supposed to look. His graying hair is clipped in a butch haircut. He sports a thin mustache. He is burly and tight-lipped and efficient. He is one of forty-three men stationed with the escort unit in Oakland. One time he almost decked a railroad agent who wanted to put an HR in with the baggage.

He had almost finished his coffee in the operations office. The man from the funeral home in Columbus had brought his son along for the ride, and they were ready to go.

"How many times have you done this?"

"This makes forty-four," Cameron said.

"It must work on your nerves."

"No. Not really. It's got to be done."

Then somebody said, "I figured they'd send 'em home on a train instead of a hearse. Hearse gets expensive."

The sergeant put down his coffee. "These men go first class," he said. "They deserve it. They've given everything a man can give." Sergeant Cameron briskly stepped outside. He checked to be sure the doors of the hearse were locked. He stepped back and gave a final salute. Then he and the driver and the driver's son got into the hearse and they drove into the night to take Sgt. Billy E. Goad home for the last time.

Off to War

The jet had just lifted off at Guam. Mrs. Langston waited until the no-smoking sign went off, and then she unfastened her seat belt and turned to the Filipino who had just taken the seat next to her and said, "Are you going to see the war?"

"The war." His name was Antonio Dimalanta.

"Of course. The war we have going on there."

Dimalanta said, "No, I go to Manila."

"Manila," said Mrs. Langston. "Is that your home?"

"Yes, but I have not been there lately." Dimalanta aleady regretted his choice of seats. "I have been in Guam for four months. I am going home for a week. Then I will go to Bangkok."

"Oh, what a coincidence. That's where I'm going. My husband is already there. He is with a large corporation. We've been in Honolulu for the last six years. We hated to leave. Honolulu is so civilized."

"What will he do in Bangkok?" said Dimalanta.

"Construction."

"Perhaps I will see you. I do the same thing."

"Is that why you've been in Guam?"

"Yes. Extending runways. The B-52s are there."

Mrs. Langston looked out the window at the Pacific, now gleaming in the sun. "The war," she said. "So ugly. It seems like we're all caught up in the war now."

We were halfway to Saigon. This is, they say, everybody's war. This one belongs to Mrs. Langston and to Tony Dimalanta. It belongs to the fat whore who had got on at Guam and was going to Manila on furlough, and to the crew-cut Navy captain headed for Da Nang in South Vietnam, and to the New York salesman drinking Scotch in the rear of the plane, and to the newsmen on board. But most of all it belongs to the young Marines and soldiers who sat in the blocked-out seats toward the back and told jokes while a sleek commercial jet streaked toward this steaming and inconsequential little country that dangles from Southeast Asia like a broken ankle.

It was eight-thirty in the morning when the plane touched down for a brief stop in Manila. Mrs. Langston and Tony Dimalanta and the whore gathered their bags and got off. In the Transit Lounge the stewardesses had hurried in and were thumbing through the souvenir linens and hemp place mats. The men crowded up to the bar, cooling off beneath ceiling fans.

"New York, you said?"

"Only city in the world," said the salesman.

"Saigon?"

"No longer than I can help it, pal. Then Tokyo."

"What do you sell?"

"Little bit of everything."

"Like what?"

"You'd never understand."

The captain came to the bar. Everybody was drinking, because the plane would board in ten minutes. "How about that," the captain said. "I buy a postcard and a stamp, gave 'em a dollar, and what do I get for change? Six cheap cigars and some Filipino cigarettes. They'll take your money, but they can't change it."

"No sweat in Saigon," the salesman said. "They'll change anything. Including your underwear."

Somebody asked the captain, "Do you fly?"

"No. Seabees. Construction."

"Where are you headed?"

"Da Nang. Building roads. After that I don't know."

"Hey," the salesman said, "how much insurance you got?"

"On me? My life?"

"Yeah. You. Going to a war zone."

"I think it's fifty thousand."

The salesman was getting belligerent. "Hah. Peanuts. Me, I got two million. Can you imagine? Two million bucks on my life."

"Pretty good vote of confidence," the Navy captain said.

"Damned right. Premium's eight thousand. They want me."

"Well, I hope they keep you."

"What's that?"

"You're going to Saigon, aren't you?"

From the air, gliding in over that sparkling ocean, it is a lovely country. At first you see the sandy part around Camranh Bay where they are building what could become one of the world's largest and busiest harbors. It is beautiful and peaceful there, seen from the air, and then the country goes lush green and there is little you can see. You can only imagine quiet hamlets and steaming banana plantations and mile-high waterfalls and stalking panthers and piranah-swirling mountain lakes. And scrawny little men wearing black pajamas and holding submachine guns and squatting in mountain caves.

The people on the plane, when told they were now over Vietnam, the place they had been reading about, craned their necks and became quiet. They looked much like people who slow down and stare when they see a wreck on the freeway. One of the stewardesses wondered aloud to another whether "transit passengers" would be allowed off the plane at Tan Son Nhut, the Saigon airport, which had become the busiest airport in the world due to military sorties. The Vietcong were bad about sitting out in the swamps surrounding Tan Son Nhut and taking pot shots at Pan American jetliners taking off and landing. "It depends," said the second stewardess, "on what kind of day it is down there."

The young woman from London was skittish. She sat next to

her girl friend from Australia—they were on the last leg of a round-the-world trip that would end in Singapore—and they were cupping hands around eyes in hopes of seeing signs of war. "I should hope, actually, that we stay on the plane," said the girl from London.

"But I think it would be interesting to see the war."

"Do they have soldiers and planes there and all?"

"I should think they would. It *is* a war, you know."

"It's really terribly awful, the war."

"Yes. But I do think it would be interesting."

It was a brief approach to Tan Son Nhut. That is putting it mildly. The commercial jets, of late, have taken to dive-bombing the landing strip and leaving the engines running and kicking out the terminal passengers and getting the hell out of there. No one was to leave the plane except those with a purpose to do so. The field bristled with armed soldiers and fighter planes and helicopters and even old C-47 "Gooney Birds." All of them were wrapped inside three-sided, sandbagged nests.

"Thank you," the head stewardess was saying over the public-address system. "And especially our military. Keep up your spirits and good luck to you all." The New York salesman bounded off the plane. Several other businessmen and newsmen followed him. The transit passengers stared in awe at the military machinery. Then they saw the young soldiers in their wrinkled uniforms as they walked grimly from the plane into the boiling heart of Saigon. Maybe this is everybody's war. But most of all it is—like other wars—a war for frightened young men in wrinkled uniforms. Scared out of their minds.

POW of the Year

Dak To, Vietnam

The captain and the major sat on rattan stools at
the bar while a big black sergeant who said he
used to spar with Bob Satterfield mixed drinks. Two officers still
wore their jungle fatigues and canvas boots. The captain was
drinking his bourbon out of one of those big fruit-jar glasses, and
he was getting into it pretty good by seven-thirty at night. They
said they had come up from Kontum earlier in the day when the
North Vietnamese soldier turned himself in.

The North Vietnamese soldier still had on his tan uniform. He
was sitting on a rattan couch facing away from the bar, sitting between a private and a South Vietnamese interpreter, and he was
working on his second can of Schlitz. He was also eating a sandwich. And waiting for the movie to start. The movie was going to
be *Monkey's Uncle*. In color. A comedy. With a big fan above the
rattan couch to keep him cool. He was certain he had made the
proper decision.

"See if the boy wants another beer," said the sergeant.

"We don't need a drunk prisoner," the major said.

"He's no prisoner now. He's one of ours."

"What the hell. Give him a beer. Loosen him up."

The bartender broke open another Schlitz and walked over to

the couch and presented the beer to the North Vietnamese. The soldier was a slim, good-looking kid with fine teeth. He smiled a very nice smile to the bartender, and when he said something to his interpreter everybody laughed.

"That boy never had it so good," the captain said.

"What's the story on him?"

"Sergeant. Squad leader. Twenty-six. Ran out on his outfit four days ago. Couldn't find anybody to turn himself in to."

"Why'd he quit?"

"Like anybody. Scared shitless. Sick, B-52s, everything."

"He ain't dumb," said the bartender.

Somebody asked, "What happens to him next?"

"We turn him over to the South Vietnamese," the major said.

"That's bad?"

"That's very bad."

"He talking?"

"He's worse than Milton Berle."

The major had just begun to explain how the next morning they would make a tape recording with the North Vietnamese turncoat when the phone rang. The bartender answered it. He said it was for either the major or the captain. The major took the phone. When he hung up he came back to the bar and ordered another drink, and he was not at all pleased.

"Don't tell me," the captain said.

"You guessed it," the major told him.

"Right now?"

"Right now. They're on their way over."

They were asked, "What's up?"

The captain said, "Psy-ops. Psychological Warfare boys. Now just why the hell can't they wait until the morning to make their tape? This boy's still gonna be around tomorrow. But no. Let's do it now, they say. Middle of the goddamn night."

Then the movie came on. A lot of people say *Monkey's Uncle* is a lousy movie. Very corny stuff. What they do not stop to consider is the alternative the turncoat had. Up in the hills maybe twenty miles away his ex-buddies were digging holes ten feet deep to get away from the 432 tons of bombs the B-52s were going to drop the next morning. He acted as though it were the best movie Hollywood ever made.

The next day, after the B-52 strike, between the hours of two and four P.M., an Army plane with a loudspeaker mounted on its side circled the area where the survivors were being methodically assassinated by U.S. ground troops. The voice you heard was that of the turncoat, the POW of the Year, from a tape made the night before. He told his brothers they should turn themselves in. He mentioned the good treatment he had received.

Mama-San

T hen there are the civilians, construction people mostly, and they come out of places like Sumiton, Alabama, and they don't really care how the war is going, because a good old boy from Sumiton never saw the kind of money you can make working one year helping build bridges, runways, roads, and barracks in Vietnam.

There was this one the other day. He was red-haired and freckle-faced. He wore a $1.98 wash-and-wear shirt and a pair of khaki Army trousers and rippled-soled boots with mud all over them, and he was getting on the elevator at the Caravelle Hotel, the class joint around here.

"Sir?" said the elevator boy at the ground floor, with all the dignity he could muster.

"Don't keer how you do it, boy, jist git me to where you chow down," this guy said.

So you had one of them sitting there at this place on Tu Do Street the other day. Tu Do has been affected by this war as has no other place you ever saw. The bars have names right out of Bourbon Street, names that would change from, say, La New York to La Frankreich tomorrow if the Germans were to move into the picture.

This place is mostly a restaurant, although it has become a profitable pickup point for some of the ladies who are seen around. It may be one of the very few places in town where you can get a hamburger and Coke and some French fries. It was five-thirty in the afternoon, and Mama-San sat at one of the tables against the back wall. She was no more than sixteen years old and pregnant again, and across from her was one of the construction boys. There were GIs at most of the other tables and they were taking it all in.

The engineer says, "I love you. You know that, don't you? I'll do anything for you."

"You very nice," said Mama-San. Her dress was white and very tight.

"Can I get you anything?"

"Baby have dirty clothes. Mama-San need box of Tide."

"I can get into the PX. You know that? I can get into the PX."

"PX very nice. Mama-San want baby to have clean clothes."

"I'll be back in a minute."

The engineer was nearly bald. That does not necessarily mean a man cannot act like a gentleman. The PX is no more than three blocks away. He ordered another Coke for Mama-San, and he got up and hurried out the open doors into the heat of Tu Do.

These women in Saigon are very tricky. You have to watch them every minute. That is where the engineer made his mistake. You could not blame him. How would he know Mama-San would say, "Whatsa mattah, somethin' wrong with your eye?"

The two GIs sitting at the table directly across from Mama-San seemed innocent enough. They wore short-sleeve sportshirts with the sleeves rolled shorter, and they were drinking Cokes and swallowing hamburgers.

"Ma'am?" the younger one said.

"Somethin' wrong with your eye?"

"I got something in it, I guess."

"You winked, GI. I know you winked. You wanna come sit with me?"

"No, ma'am. Uh-uh, baby, not me." The other GI thought that was funny.

Mama-San howled. Mama-San got up and wiggled toward the

jukebox in her tight white dress with her stomach pouching out, and when she did that all of the soldiers stopped eating their hamburgers to watch. She joked with the two near the jukebox as she put on a tune called "A Fool Never Learns," and then she went back to the table and the engineer came through the door and sat down again with her. He had a brown package, one of those packages from the PX.

"Mama-San thank you," she said.

"You're really something, baby," he told her, passing the package across the table.

Air-conditioned War

Saigon

You never know what it is going to be like. Most of the time it is a matter of working like a computer. You are shown a map and given the coordinates, and somebody out on the flight line loads your bird with napalm and rockets and rounds of bullets, and you have a briefing and get in the air and unload your arsenal when your charts show you are over the proper target, and within two hours you are back home on the ground drinking coffee, and if somebody asks you what the war is like, you do not know, because yours is a computer war.

Sure, sometimes it is different. There are always exceptions. Sometimes you prowl around like a buzzard, as if in a World War I dogfight, and that is when you are able to go back to Operations and drink coffee while your nerves jitterbug and you have something to talk about. But most of the time it is a computer war, flying a jet fighter over Vietnam.

Capt. Scott Freeman had dressed in the dark in the apartment he shares with the other pilots in Saigon, and by six o'clock in the morning he was walking into the operations room of the 416th Tactical Fighter Squadron at Tan Son Nhut Air Base in Saigon. He wore his pale-green flight suit, with a patch on the chest saying

THE SILVER KNIGHTS. He carried a Thermos filled with hot black coffee. He is a short, slight man, going on twenty-eight, with a four-year-old daughter back in the States.

He has been flying a F-100-F Supersabre jet fighter in Vietnam for five months now. He has made nearly a hundred sorties in that time. This morning he was making another.

At six-thirty-five Capt. Lyle Beckers gathered the other young pilots around a table in the operations room. They sat in chairs. It was still dark and foggy on the runway outside, but the pilots were wide-eyed. All of them were young Air Force captains. There was Beckers, the flight leader, and Pat Swenson and J. J. Simms and Scott Freeman.

"We'll check the time," Beckers said first. "Six-thirty-five."

"Six-thirty-five."

"This is mission number 47634. We'll start engines at seven-thirty and take off at eight."

The others took notes on the pads they would strap around their thighs in the planes.

Beckers gave the target. It was a Vietcong concentration about 110 miles east of Tan Son Nhut. The 101st Airborne Division was operating there on a search-and-destroy operation called Austin II. The village was near Phan Thiet.

"After I get rid of my napalm," Beckers was saying, "I'll come back up. If we've got anything of importance, we'll strafe. Try not to get below five hundred feet, and don't strafe if you don't have to."

"At two-fifty a round, that's smart," somebody said.

"If somebody gets hit, the guy behind him looks him over. If somebody gets out of an airplane up there, the guy behind him should stay close and see where he lands. Emergency fields, use Phan Rang. Then we've got Bien Hoa."

The four pilots methodically climbed into their gear. Their gear included knives and emergency first-aid kits and flares and pistols and Mae West life jackets and, of course, parachutes. They walked briskly to the flight line and got into their planes.

"Where you headed, Cap'n?" said Dudley, the young crew chief who has been with Freeman since they served together in England.

"Gonna get a cup of coffee up around Camranh Bay," Scott Freeman said.

Then they got into their planes, sleek camouflaged jets that cost $700,000 apiece and dart through the skies like crazy sparrows, and they waited in line to take off from the busiest airport in the world, and suddenly they were aloft and in formation, speeding effortlessly toward another of those anonymous target areas with their napalm pods clinging to their wings like cocoons on a tree limb.

This is Scott Freeman's life. His father is a lieutenant colonel at MacDill Air Force Base, in Tampa. Scott's father wanted him to finish college, but he quit after one semester at Texas A&M and joined the Air Force as an enlisted man at the age of nineteen.

He became crew chief on a B-47. He applied for the Aviation Cadet program and won his wings. He has been stationed in Europe, and this is his second tour of duty in Vietnam.

He has flown eleven missions in a vulnerable single-engine spotter plane over Vietnam in addition to his one hundred missions in the snazzy F-100-F during this tour. A few days ago he had a feeler from an international commercial airline, which promised him that in a very short time he would be earning nearly thirty thousand dollars a year.

He could take the job right now, and in three years he would make as much as a major, and it will be more than a year before he is even put up for major. He turned the job down.

"It's been rough for my wife," he says. "I don't see how she takes it, my being gone all the time. It's my life. It sounds corny, but it's a love of flying and being around the greatest bunch of guys anywhere. You learn to be aggressive, cocky, an individual.

"It's different than in the infantry. You don't take anybody's word for anything. You learn it'll save your life one day to be like that. And yet I've seen more teamwork—teamwork you wouldn't believe—especially from a bunch of individuals like us. War stinks anytime, and this one stinks longer than any of the others. I've been in the hospital three times already from stuff like food poisoning.

"This war's put ten years on my life. But I need to be here. This country, you get the people organized, with the natural resources they have, it would rival Japan in thirty years."

The eastern shore is the most beautiful part of this beautiful country. It sticks its head out of the blue-green water like a blond mermaid, strolls a short distance through dark green forests, and then races up into heavily wooded hills that meet the clouds. We were three miles above this country when the radio began to crackle. An American Forward Air Controller, a single-engine plane that flits over the treetops and plays third-base coach on all Tactical Air Command operations, was miles away and looking for help. He was homing in a South Vietnamese B-57 pilot on a small village in the foothills.

"Okay, Seven-two, I want you to come west. Two-seven-oh," the FAC said over the radio.

"Okay," the Vietnamese said.

"Do not drop short. Repeat, do not drop short."

"Okay, I see it."

"All right. Now. You see it, to the right of the road? Drop your napalm in the trenches. That's where they are, to the right of the road, in the trenches."

"There it is, right there."

"Roger. Okay, boy, go in and get 'em."

"Sounds like they got a good one going," Captain Freeman said.

Scott Freeman and the other three American pilots in their F-100-Fs had heard it. The FAC had asked for help, and they had diverted from their primary target and sped to the scene. When they flew over the top of the steep mountains above the village, they saw smoke spiraling from the valley below.

"That's a good picture," Freeman said. American soldiers were closing in on the village. The Vietcong were heading for the hills. Bright orange flames licked out from the trees.

The Vietnamese in the B-57 had run out of time and ammunition. He had done a hell of a job of softening up. Now the F-100-Fs would drive in and take the Vietcong's mind off the infantrymen rushing down the narrow dirt road.

"Very nice, very nice," the FAC told the Vietnamese pilot, now pulling out of the valley.

"Roger," Captain Beckers said. "We're gonna make a run."

"Right. You see where the last one hit? Go in and drop your napalm there. Remember, don't shoot anything north of the road."

"Here we go."

The lead plane, Beckers's jet, peeled off and suddenly dived into the valley. The world begins to spin in a dive. From above, it appeared that he had been hit and was heading straight into the trees. He leveled off.

He released his napalm bombs. Both of them flipped lazily from the wings and tumbled end over end until they hit the trees and burst into flames, licking up everything in their path.

The other jets came behind him. When we had dropped our load, we shot straight up to meet God.

The Vietcong were on the run now. They were running for the hills. The soldiers had watched it all, and now they were charging into the village. We straightened out of our dive, circled the village, and found the dirt trail leading up the mountain. The people, both sides, looked like ants.

"Everybody stand high and dry," Captain Beckers said over the radio. Then he peeled off again. We followed. We dropped our napalms, and the blue-green mountainside turned to a heaving orange, and we jerked out of the dive and headed home and left the whole lousy, stinking mess to the people down in the valley.

It was so peaceful, coming home. We had Patti Page singing "Basin Street" on the radio. The traffic was stacked up at Tan Son Nhut, so Captain Beckers waggled his plane and we formed into trail formation and followed him in a few rolls, as playful as drunken dolphins.

Saigon is much prettier at ten thousand feet. We got back into formation, and Captain Beckers peeled off and landed and we came right in on his tail, and when you opened the canopy and took off your oxygen mask, the heat brought you back to earth, and the first thing Scott Freeman said when Dudley put the yellow ladder up to the cockpit was, "What time is it?"

"Ten o'clock."

"Too late for breakfast again."

So we had coffee from the Thermos bottle in Operations, and it wasn't bad at all, and tomorrow we will probably go out and drop our garbage like computers and come back and wonder how the war is going. It is much more pleasant to think about how it went today, when you could actually see them trying to run into the hills.

Policing the Area

Dak To

You could not tell whether he was young or old, because he had been lying there in the mud for four
days and his skin had turned black and maggots were crawling out
of his mouth. He was an elite North Vietnamese soldier, though,
and everybody knew that, because they had sent nothing but the
best—spewing them up and over the mountains from Laos and
Cambodia—for the summer push. They had won some and they
had lost some. This one had not been so lucky. He had undoubt-
edly killed a lot of soldiers by the time the Americans, with their
artillery and B-52 strikes and helicopters, killed him at his
machine-gun post in a cave in the central highlands halfway between Hanoi and Saigon.

And now the sun was straight up, and A-Company, 2nd Battal-
ion, 502 Infantry, 101st Airborne division, had finally taken the
hill, and what was so bad was the smell of seven enemy bodies
with thousands of maggots and flies and mosquitoes swarming
over them.

First Sgt. Kenneth Lamb came over to the company com-
mander, Capt. Ronald Brown, of Chattanooga, Tennessee. Both
of them were grimy with mud and sweat. The sweat was streaming down out of their helmets and streaking their faces with mud.

"They just found another one over the hill, sir," Sergeant Lamb told Captain Brown.

"Good. Another old one?"

"Yessir. I figure about four days old. All of 'em about four days in here. Looks like the artillery got 'em the night after we got hit. They were really dug in."

"Okay. Good. Police the weapons. Make it to the top."

Sergeant Lamb looked at the North Vietnamese soldier's body sprawled out where he had died. The body smelled like dead fish. "Sir?" he said to Lieutenant Brown.

"Yes?"

"This boy is really gonna smell."

"So?"

"It looks like we're gonna be here awhile."

"Okay," said Lieutenant Brown. "Cover him up. Throw some dirt."

"Yessir. Thank you, sir."

They had been two hours making it from the landing zone in the valley. The helicopters had dropped them there in the morning at eight o'clock, and it had taken until ten o'clock to move four hundred yards through the bamboo because the North Vietnamese had left two dozen men behind to cover their tracks. A-Company had killed them all in a brisk firefight without having a single one of theirs hurt. And now they were on top of the first ridge, and the dirty work of looking for bodies and weapons was going to occupy them for the next several hours. The men were scouring the area, and when they would find a canteen or a body or a weapon they would bring it back to the bomb crater and spread the spoils on the ground in the sun so somebody could make out a report on what had been found.

Capt. Ronald Brown took a sip of water from his canteen. He is twenty-six years old and has been in Vietnam for four months. He had played freshman football at Georgia Tech before flunking out. Then he enrolled at West Point and graduated in 1962. He will make a career of the Army. "This is the dirty work, cleaning up like this," he was saying, "but it does the kids a lot of good.

These are the same guys who chopped us up the other day when we had to get in and relieve Charlie Company."

"How many did you lose in that one?"

"Two killed, five wounded."

"How does it feel?"

"What?"

"Commanding. Losing people."

Brown drank more water and wiped his forehead with his sleeves. "Since this operation began, ten days ago, I've lost seven and had twenty-three wounded. It's no fun. The worst thing about this job is seeing these kids get hurt."

The men were still finding bodies and weapons. All of the bodies were blackened and rotting. They had been killed at their guns. It was going to be a big haul. The men had already found two mortars and dozens of other, smaller weapons. They were not jubilant as they brought them out of the bushes and spread them out on the ground near the bomb crater. There is nothing about war that makes a man jubilant. Not even killing a man who killed your buddies four hours earlier.

"Sir," one of them said, "they found a cave."

"Get a man with a rope and a shotgun," said Brown.

"Yessir."

"Tell him to be careful."

"Yessir."

"I won't take all of the gooks in the world for one man."

"Yessir," Brown was told.

Now they were throwing dirt over the dead enemy soldier. The maggots and the flies were confused. They swarmed over the smooth mound of dirt. One of the men who had been covering the body came up to the captain and showed him what he had found in the enemy soldier's pockets. There was a pocket Bible in English and a sample package of Lucky Strikes and a packet of C-rations and a slender book of coupons.

"What's that?" the captain said.

"Bible? That's a Gideon."

"Naw. The booklet."

The soldier opened it up. It was a payment booklet from a loan company in Fayetteville, North Carolina, and one of the others guessed it represented payments for a car. The American had made nine payments of twenty-five dollars each. The next payment was due in five weeks.

"Charlie Company?" one of them said.

"Charlie Company."

"Shit."

"Poor sumbitch. Ahead in his payments."

One of the men stuck the booklet in his pocket. They were silent as they trudged back into the bamboo and went back to their work.

A Flag on the Square

Fayetteville, Georgia

I t was a raw morning, and the sky was as gray as the Fayette County courthouse. The building stands in the center of the square, as courthouses do in small towns all over the south. When a gust of wind came it would nudge the yellow leaves from the gnarled trees, and the leaves would drift until they settled on the long, green winter grass of the courthouse lawn. The only sounds came from the big tractor-trailer rigs groaning and shifting down and trying to make the light. They were on their way to Atlanta and they do not stop in Fayetteville.

The four Marines who had come down from Atlanta to form the color guard wore their bright-blue dress uniforms and carried rifles, and they were rehearsing the flag-raising ceremony while the people stood on the sidewalk. The sidewalk curves around the new flagpole and the modest marble monument at its base. The monument reads IN MEMORY OF FAYETTE COUNTIANS WHO LOST THEIR LIVES WHILE SERVING IN THE ARMED FORCES IN VIET NAM. There was one small brass plate beneath that. It read PFC. TOM E. BOREN USMC, JUNE 10, 1966, DA NANG, SOUTH VIET NAM.

"I didn't know the boy myself," said one of the men standing on the sidewalk. They spoke in low voices.

"They haven't lived here long."

"It doesn't matter anyway," another man said. "He's from here. This is a good thing, the monument and the flagpole."

The first man said, "I hope it's the last name we have to put on there. The first and the last."

By a few minutes past eleven o'clock everyone was in place. The people who would take part in the ceremony sat in wooden folding chairs on a rickety platform behind the flagpole. In the front row were Mr. and Mrs. Earl Boren. Mrs. Boren wore an olive dress and held a new American flag folded in her lap. The people across the street at Ward's Pharmacy came out and watched from the sidewalk when they heard the Fayette County High School band start playing "My Country 'Tis of Thee." And that is how, on Friday, November 11, this lousy war ten thousand miles away came to Fayetteville, Georgia.

Tom Boren was nineteen. He was born and reared in Bessemer, Alabama, but his family had moved to Fayette County about two years ago. His brother, John, was two years older and had gone into the Marine Corps in September of 1964. When Tom Boren graduated from Forest Park High School last year, he worked for a while but then decided to enlist in the Marines. That was late last December.

It happened very quickly. He went off to boot camp at Parris Island and then to Camp Lejeune, North Carolina, for advanced training. Then, on May 29 of this year, he left for South Vietnam. He arrived at Da Nang on June 6 and was assigned to a platoon in the First Marine Division the next day. His brother was on reconnaissance patrol near the Laotian border, so they did not have a chance to get together. On June 8 Pfc. Tom Boren's outfit moved into the jungle. He was killed in action on June 10, the first Fayette Countian to lose his life in the Vietnam War.

The ceremony on the courthouse lawn was brief and tasteful. About a hundred people, many of them young ones who had known Tom Boren, were gathered around the flagpole. Mrs. Boren handed a sergeant the flag. The band played the "Marine Hymn." Then the drums began to roll, and a freckle-faced little red-haired boy rose up out of the band and put a trumpet to his lips and blew taps. The flag was raised, and Mrs. Boren had a green handkerchief at her mouth and sat motionless now, and there was the "Star Spangled Banner" and it was almost done.

"We are here today to honor one who followed the flag." It was Grady Huddleston, the principal speaker. His voice came out of the two speakers mounted in windows on the second floor of the courthouse. It echoed through the quiet, empty streets.

"It cannot and it will not be said that he died in vain. Let us rededicate ourselves that as long as we have one man fighting for our flag, we will back him one hundred percent. . . . The reality comes to those who suffer the great personal tragedy. Let us on this day and every day following realize that there is this great, ugly ideology that will stop at nothing. . . ."

A white wreath was laid on the monument. The benediction was given. The people spoke quietly to one another, and the kids in the band piled back into the yellow school bus on the square, and suddenly the square was empty. The new American flag opened up and fluttered in the soft breeze, like a bird learning to fly.

On the Road

"If you're drinking to try and forget, please remember to pay your tab in advance."

Plaque in a Nevada roadside saloon

*B*y now I have lost count of the number of places where I have lived. I can remember Boston and Paris and Atlanta and San Francisco. I can remember also, because of their particular shabbiness, the villa in Vietnam and the barracks at Lackland Air Force Base in San Antonio and the dollar-a-day rooming house in Montgomery and the free upstairs room in a little town in southeast Kansas where once I played baseball. Each, in its own time, served its purpose. It probably comes out to one domicile per year over the twenty years since I fled the house where I grew up.

We Southerners of my generation are the first to be able to say that we ran away from home. The ones before us always kind of hung around the place. It was unspeakable for them to announce abruptly, "Well, I'll be leaving for St. Louis 'bout Friday." We were the first of our kin down home to get educated and make some money and be able to buy a bus ticket to all of those exotic jobs. So we did it, in all of our newfound mobility, and we rode off to Chicago and Kansas City and Los Angeles and New York. And we found a whole new world waiting out there, where the waitress in a diner didn't wipe her nose with her sleeve and blurt Whatchallwant? and where they talked funny and where you actually had people with dark skin driving taxicabs. "What in the world," we would ask on our first visit, "is a taxicab, anyway?"

My old man used to drive the other men of the family crazy when they were *sitting around in the parlor smoking cigars and waiting for Mama Nelson to finish with the mashed potatoes. He had just come in off the road, having driven his truck to Texas and back, and they knew it and he knew it. Uncle Lacey hung around an office all week to sell Prudential insurance. Another uncle, the crazed inventor, lay back on the grass at Inman Yards trying to envision new ways to switch boxcars for Southern Railway. "Yeah, boy," my old man would tell them, "that Fort Worth. That Fort Worth's a wild place." I think that is why I hitchhiked to Missouri when I was a teenager.*

Hitching

Anywhere, U.S.A.

Hitchhiking, thumb up on some dusty road with the diesels honking and the curious kids in the back of the station wagons blinking their eyes, was the only way to go. By Friday, after a week of sneaking beer at the roadside joints and paying for a couple of movies and buying some hamburgers and cigarettes, a college student was flat out of money. The only way to get home for the weekend—home, where Daddy and the bank account were—was to go out on the road and beg. GIVE A STUDENT A LIFT read the sign on the cozy bus shelter at every road leading out of town. There was another reason for hitching, too, although we never discovered it until after the fact. We found out that hitching rides was a good way to get an education. This was not, as Merle Haggard sings in "I Take a Lot of Pride in What I Am," the sort of education you get in a classroom. College professors who read from notes they have been using for twenty years cannot tell you how it is Out There. They can tell you that two plus two equals four, but they can't tell you *why*. And that is the only thing that really counts. *Why?*

One time in Arkansas, just west of Memphis, I was stranded on a stark stretch of blacktop for three hours. It was almost impossible during the 1950s to get a ride around there because of the pub-

licity attending the murder of a family by some crazy who stuffed
them all in a well after getting a ride from them in their station
wagon. Finally, at dawn, a farmer in a pickup truck stopped. I had
to ride in the back with two hogs. He stopped about ten miles
down the road, in the middle of nowhere, and let me out. An hour
later I got a ride with a crazy old woman, about eighty, who had
three dozen gallon bottles of "water" in the back of her Model T.
It took an hour for us to move ten miles. She stopped at nearly
every dirt road leading off the blacktop. She had no teeth, and her
hair was bailing out. After every delivery she would return to the
Model T stuffing bills into her smock. When it appeared I was
getting impatient she invited me to drink some of the water. It was
probably the best moonshine whiskey I ever tasted.

Hitching was, then, the most educational experience I ever had.
You found out how Real People lived. You encountered drifters
and families allegedly off on carefree vacations and bug-eyed
truckers and frenetic traveling salesmen. Hitching, even once we
had graduated from college and had enough money to buy plane
and bus tickets, was a nostalgic trip worth every minute of the ef-
fort. It was the "call of the open road." It was like kissing a girl for
the first time. You figured that the stories about hitchhikers being
molested—beaten, robbed, raped—by drivers were as overplayed
as the stories about airplane crashes. You figured that thousands
of hitchhikers were being picked up each day without incident,
just as millions of people were flying in planes without crashing,
and that the occasional mayhem that took place was happen-
stance.

All of that, however, was before a certain summer in Missouri.
This was around 1955. For two summers I had been playing
semipro baseball in southeastern Kansas. The minute college let
out in Alabama I would hitchhike the eight hundred or so miles to
Kansas, in order to save money (my salary was fifty dollars a week,
and I got free room and board), and when the season ended I
would hitch back home to Birmingham before the new term
began. There had been some moments of trepidation during that
period—a homosexual approach at a bus depot in Jonesboro, a

terrible accident in Corinth, Mississippi—but in general the plan had worked. I had always got where I needed to get. For free.

It was hot that day, blistering hot, as only Missouri can get in August. This was at the edge of the Ozarks, where there are low, ugly mounds of red dirt. After two hours of beating off the gnats at the split in the road, I saw him coming. I had been there for more than two hours. Coming toward me was a faded-green Terraplane Hudson, which you don't see anymore (there is, today, a Terraplane society celebrating one of the last of the ugliest American automobiles), but at this point I would take a ride in a Sherman tank.

The driver was a burly man. He hadn't shaved in two or three days. His hair was mussed. It was so hot he had taken off his shirt. His sleeveless undershirt was soaked with sweat. Ugly black hair covered his arms and his shoulders like a sweater. He drove with his left hand. He kept his right hand on the seat, under the shirt between us. He didn't say much. I was scared to death.

"Hot, ain't it?" I said.

"You got that part right," he said.

"How far you going?"

"Where you *want* to go?"

"Springfield."

"Then I'm going to Springfield."

He kept looking at me without saying anything. He never moved his hand from beneath the shirt on the seat. I made jokes, but he would only smile faintly. He asked me where I was going and where I had been. I told him I had been playing baseball and was going back home to return to college. I told him I loved my mother and I wanted to be a writer if I couldn't be a baseball player. "Uh-huh," he said. Then he moved his hand from beneath the shirt and a pistol flashed, and I learned, for the first time, that it works both ways. "I guess you're all right," he said. "Put this in the glove compartment, will you?" He even bought my lunch at the next roadside diner. It was the last time I hitchhiked.

Truck Stop

Valdosta, Georgia

It was only halfway through the morning in South Georgia, but already the steam was beginning to rise from the asphalt on the highway. You could stand on the side of the road and see it. The big trucks, hauling watermelons out of Florida or headed for Tampa with heavy loads of automobile tires, were making time before the sun got any higher and made driving unbearable. They were whizzing north and south on the highway, and when they would pass, you saw them jolt each other with the wind forced out of the way by their bulk and their speed, and the steam that rose from the pavement stirred when they passed, as when a sudden breeze hits a wheat field in Kansas.

Smokestacks on top of the huge diesels cut through the air like submarine periscopes knifing the water, the black smoke coming in ugly puffs. There's one from California. And one out of Texas. And Miami, and Detroit, and Akron. Big trucks, little trucks, diesels and gas jobs. Signs on the left-rear sides of their trailers saying PASSING SIDE, and signs on the right saying SUI-SIDE.

The drivers, in the stifling heat, are already stripped down to their undershirts. They are wearing General MacArthur caps with the pliant bills curved on the sides to protect their eyes from the glare of the windshield, and under the caps are wraparound Air

Force sunglasses. And they are hunched over the steering wheels, looking for the next hill, and all of them are trying to eat up as much highway as they can before the heat gets so bad they have to pull in at a truck stop and rest their rigs as you would a tired horse.

Pete's place sits beside the road on a long and flat stretch, and he doesn't go in much for advertising. He doesn't have to. One mile down the highway in both directions, Pete has little home-made signs saying GAS–EATS–COFFEE, and that is all the advertising necessary. You make a good cup of coffee, the drivers find out about it on their own and pass the word: That is the way you advertise a truck stop. Good coffee, good conversation, and plenty of room to park your rig. That's the trick.

Inside, Pete and Louise have all they could handle. Three drivers are straddling stools at the counter, drinking hot, black coffee from heavy white mugs chipped and scarred with age. In the corner booth two more drivers have their elbows around plates heaped with bacon and scrambled eggs, and they are not sparing the time to talk with anyone until they are finished.

Louise wears a white uniform, and her long black hair is gathered at the back with a bright-red ribbon tied in a bow, and she looks up from pouring boiling water into the huge coffee urn when she hears the huge red diesel leave the highway and crunch over the gravel outside. The driver parks his rig next to the trees, gets out, and stretches his legs, checks his tires, and then walks toward the door.

He is a lean and tall man with bronze skin and shiny black hair. He opens the weathered screen door with a large, rough hand, pushes his cap back, and takes off his wraparound sunglasses, and when he smiles, all you see is a row of teeth stained yellow from chewing cigars.

"Well, well, well, if it ain't my buddy Tex," Louise says when the driver has taken a stool at the counter.

"Sugar, I been driving since midnight just to have breakfast with you," Tex replies.

"I bet you said that this morning to the last one."

Tex orders a platter of ham and eggs. He mops his forehead

with a red polka-dot bandanna and sticks his face in front of a small fan suspended from the plaster pillar holding up the ceiling in the middle of the room. When Louise stands on her toes to pour another pot of boiling water over the coffee, he leans over the counter to steal a look at her calves.

"Where you headed?" Louise asks him.

"Kentucky," he says. "Got watermelons."

"Haven't had a watermelon since last August."

"It's about that time again. You still married?"

"Now, that's a fresh line for you, ain't. it?" Louise said. " 'Course I ain't married. It ain't my cup o' tea, so to speak."

"Maybe taking a little trip to Kentucky with ol' Tex is, then."

"Don't think your wife would like that, sugar. Here. Here's your breakfast. Down the hatch, tiger."

Tex tears into the ham and eggs, and now Pete's place is quiet again. Pete draws himself a cup of coffee and drinks it while he straightens the comic postcards on the glass counter next to the cash register. Louise finishes pouring boiling water into the coffee urn. And outside you can see the big trucks and the little trucks jostling each other as they pass on the highway, smoke belching from the smokestacks and screams coming from pebbles stuck in the tire treads as they run away from the hot South Georgia sun.

See America First

Eureka, Nevada

You aren't going to believe the Colonnade Hotel, one block off the main drag, which is U.S. Highway 50, in Eureka. That is eureka as in "I have found it." The travel writers would call Eureka a "quaint mining town hidden amid the craggy wilds of the Great American West." Why the hell anybody would live in Eureka I will never know. Somebody once described a scraggly Florida Panhandle town to me as a place where nobody ever stops on purpose. All I know is, one of the most honored regular patrons of the Colonnade Hotel is a gray-bearded and odorous, bow-legged old prospector who comes down out of the hills once a month and slaps two dollars on the desk for the privilege—no, the duty—of taking a hot shower. Eureka, I bet, boasts of some of the most sensuous sheep in America.

Anyway, this lady and I more or less collided with Eureka. We had been on the road for three or four days—Tallahassee, Birmingham, Memphis, Kansas, Colorado, Utah—and now, at dusk, we actually saw some signs of life in the bowels of Nevada.

"Neon," said my relief driver.

"Neon what?"

"Neon lights," she said. "Civilization. Folks. Coors beer."

The lady, now, it must be understood, has a working relationship with American Tacky. It doesn't really make much sense. For forty hours each week she edits articles for the Florida Department of Commerce about alligators and "reptile institutes" and sandy beaches and high-rise condominiums, all the time becoming nauseated at the clutter of such phrases as "sun-glinted dwellings reaching toward the blue Florida sky" and "beaches swept by friendly Gulf winds" and the like, but she turns out to be a Holiday Inn freak. When *Sports Illustrated* published a piece two months ago about Florida's "Tacky Triangle"—that area inside Tampa and Orlando and Miami that contains all the snake farms and chalk-pink flamingos and porpoise shows one could need in a lifetime—she clandestinely made more photocopies of it than the *Tallahassee Democrat* issues papers in a single day.

"I want me a Holiday Inn," she said as we neared Eureka.
"Would a Howard Johnson's do?"
"Holiday Inn. And a Coors. And a Magic-Fingers bed."
"A Magic-Fingers."
"These vibrating beds. They do great things for your body."
"Jesus."
"And I want me a slot machine and a cheeseburger, and a color TV. You think you can handle all of that, kid?"

There is no Holiday Inn in Eureka. They have never heard of Holiday Inn in Eureka. They would not *like* Holiday Inn in Eureka. They have a couple of mom-'n-pop motels there, where you have to go up the street to the Shell station to beg ice, and then they have the Colonnade. "Yep, full up," said a kid at one of the motels, going out to hang the no-vacancy sign just as these stragglers from Tallahassee sputtered up. "Might try the Colonnade. They've *always* got rooms. You aren't gonna try to make it all the way to San Francisco in *that*, are you?"

And so here we are at the Colonnade Hotel in Eureka ("Man and *wife?*" said the lady at the desk). Those are not *odors* drifting up from the kitchen, where the Chicano owners have an apartment on the first floor; they are freaking *smells*. Nine bucks a night. Extra blankets, as an amenity, since the tourist season has begun.

Slots and hamburgers and Coors across the street at the Owl. A blinking neon light outside the window, just above the Eureka Historical Society plaque proclaiming the Colonnade as a Nevada landmark. "Maybe I'll say my prayers before I go to sleep," said Miss Holiday Inn.

Jesus, this country is big. I should have known that, having begun riding up it and down it and across it in my old man's truck when I turned twelve, but there is nothing like a cross-country drive at middle age when you think you have been some places and know some things. Eureka, Nevada, truly becomes an ant on the atlas when you have been mugged in New York and got drunk in Chicago and become lost in Kansas and been loved in Utah and been wiped out in Tahoe. The size of America is so boggling, once you hunker down to caressing it with your tires, that you get down to playing frivolous games with it. "My God," the lady from Tallahassee said, having never strayed west of New Orleans, "isn't that an amber wave of grain?" She would later say, as the miles whipped past, "Look, a purple mountain's majesty," and, "My goodness, it's a wind-whipped mountain pass."

She maybe took it too far, though, in the Ozarks of northwestern Arkansas. We stopped at a mile-high pass on the promise of being able to buy "authentic Ozark handicrafts." This friendly old nester sat behind a cash register, surrounded by chalk figurines and arrowheads and picture postcards. Fondling a particularly tacky chalk bust of an Indian chief who had once supposedly roamed the hills, she turned it over and discovered a sticker that read MADE IN TAIWAN, $9.50.

"Have you lived in Arkansas long?" she said.

"Born here," said the nester.

"I bet you know just about every town in the state."

"Name one, I been there."

"Taiwan," she said. "Taiwan, Arkansas."

"Don't think I ever heard of Taiwan. Reckon that might be up around Fayetteville. Got a lot of foreigners up that way."

Love, of a Sort

Atlanta

He had slept through most of the morning, and because he was so groggy from sleep he gave up the idea of doing any writing that day. In the afternoon, after making himself a bologna sandwich for lunch, he walked up the street and had a couple of beers at the neighborhood tavern. And now it was almost five-thirty in the afternoon, and soon she would be home with a bottle of bourbon and some Luckys. A couple of his pals had dropped by. He sat on the floor of the apartment—this apartment she was paying the rent on with her salary at the police department—playing poker and waiting for her to come home from work.

The door to the apartment opened. She was right on time. She was startled for a moment when she saw his two buddies in the living room at that time of day, but she smiled at them and came on into the room and hung her coat in the closet.

"Hi, sweet," she said.

"Where the hell you been?" he said. He was dealing.

"Oh, it was the traffic."

"You get some liquor?"

"Of course." She tossed him the pack of cigarettes and pulled the bottle of bourbon out of the brown paper bag. "Cigarettes and bourbon for my baby."

"Don't talk about it. Just pour it."

She said, "You can at least say you're glad I'm home."

"Pour, kid."

She poured four drinks from the fresh bottle of whiskey and gave a drink to him and the other two. He was still sitting in the middle of the floor, playing cards. He had not looked at her since she had first come in. She went into the kitchen with her own drink of bourbon, in a motel-room tumbler, and started making spaghetti for dinner. When she had slopped a pile of vermicelli into a kettle of boiling water and salted it, she said, still in the kitchen, "How'd the writing go today?"

"Couple of pages," he said.

"How many does that make now?"

"I didn't count 'em up yet."

"Can I see what you've done so far?"

He was laughing with his buddies. He had won the last hand. "It's bad luck," he said. "Never show somebody a piece until you've finished it. Everybody knows that. It's bad luck."

"You didn't write anything today." She was wiping her hands.

"What's that?"

"I don't believe you worked today."

"Get off my back."

"You sat and waited for me to bring you booze and cigarettes."

"You talk too goddamn much."

"But, honey, I'm interested in your welfare."

"Pour me another drink," he said. "Glass got a hole in it."

They didn't speak during dinner. He wasn't hungry. He drank the bourbon instead. She talked about her day at the office. He would butt in and talk about big card games he had dealt during his years, before he settled down, on the road hustling pool and cards and golf. The two friends of his, who had stayed for dinner, hunched over their plates of spaghetti and tried to stay out of it. After dinner they started up the poker again in the center of the living-room floor, so she went down the hall for nearly an hour to see the girl who was married. When she came back her eyes were red from crying and she was beginning to feel the bourbon she had drunk.

"I don't know what to do with him," she said to one of the men.

"Leave him out of it," he said. "He's a friend of mine."

She kept talking to the friend anyway. "I bring him everything he needs. I pay the rent. I cook. I love him. When he's sick I try to take care of him. I *love* him. What's wrong with me? I know I'm fat. But I *love* him. Can't he love me? It's the least he can do." She was out of control now, sobbing and blowing her nose into her skirt.

He broke in. "I can't hear myself think with all that shit."

"Okay. I'll stop."

Three weeks later he left. He called one of his pals at three o'clock in the morning, when she was snoring and he was loaded on whiskey, and the pal came and they threw his stuff into the trunk of the car and drove away. After that he stopped drinking so much and she found somebody else. It was, while it lasted, a funny kind of love.

Mister Ham's Overcoat

Atlanta

T he whole world is running off to Miami for the Christmas holidays. Look around and you will have cause to wonder why all of these cities and towns even bothered to string colored lights above their streets and put lighted trees in their parks, because when Christmas Day comes there is not going to be anybody here to enjoy them. Everybody is going to be in Miami. Last week it was Willie Cue, of Baltimore, who stopped off on his way down long enough to have his Christmas savings lifted by another, more clever pool shark. And this week it was Mister Ham, General Delivery, United States.

They say a lot of these traveling men are nothing but bums, but that is one thing they will never say about Mister Ham, because Mister Ham wears a dark-blue suit and a bow tie and gold cuff links and also has a pencil-thin gray mustache. And if that is not enough class for you, Mister Ham also wears a speckled overcoat that has the inscription FRANKLIN SIMON, FIFTH AVENUE, NEW YORK on the label inside, a reminder of the good years. That is, Mister Ham had his Franklin Simon overcoat as late as three o'clock Wednesday afternoon.

"Maybe you need a good overcoat for Christmas," Mister Ham was saying.

"Thought about it, but I've got one already," he was told.

"Cheap," he said. "Real cheap."

The reason Mister Ham was considering disposing of his Franklin Simon overcoat Wednesday had nothing to do with the fact that it will be so warm in Miami he won't need it. The real reason Mister Ham was taking bids was, to be perfectly blunt, because he needed the money. Mister Ham in need of cash: That is something a lot of people will not believe.

Mister Ham was born sixty years ago, the only son of a very prosperous insurance man. Just because he was the only son did not mean he was the favorite son, and it was at the age of twenty that Mister Ham officially became a black sheep by striking out from his hometown to see the rest of the world. He hit Honolulu, fell in love with San Francisco, had a big job pushing medicine in New York, took in Alaska, made money, lost money, worked for a religious organization in Texas, and, finally, wound up in very poor condition of all kinds.

"I've got four big problems," says Mister Ham. "One is emphysema, two is sinus trouble, three is my eyes, and four is I'm stupid. Either I'm stupid or everybody else is smart. I don't know which."

One guy Mister Ham claims is smart is the attorney at the bank where they took over the will of Mister Ham's mother, who passed away last year. It was May when his mother died. Nobody bothered to tell Mister Ham about it until the following August. By then it was too late for him, the only son, to do anything about the will. They had sold the property his mother owned and started sending him fifty dollars every month for the rest of his life, and being at the age of sixty, Mister Ham thinks he would prefer having all of the fifteen thousand right now instead of fifty at a time.

He sat in a short-order restaurant Wednesday, Mister Ham did, with class spilling all over him right down to the gold cuff links, sipping hot coffee and rationing cigarettes and holding his Franklin Simon overcoat on his lap. It was cold and wet outside, and when Mister Ham was told it was cold and wet outside, he said, "If it's bad for you, think what it's like for me."

"It'll be better in Miami," he was told.

"If I ever get there," he said.

"Got a job lined up?"

"Telephone work. Telephone subscriptions. When you're talking on the telephone nobody can tell you're sixty years old."

And it was sad, very sad, to be with Mister Ham Wednesday afternoon. The guy at the hotel was holding his bag because Mister Ham couldn't pay his bill. He was going to have to start hitchhiking to Miami before it got dark. He had a dollar fifty and not even a razor, and here it was, ten days before Christmas, and like everyone else Mister Ham was going to Florida so he could at least be warm.

"You've got to have some money," he was told.

With all the dignity he could muster Mister Ham straightened his shoulders and stood up and neatly folded his Franklin Simon overcoat over one arm. He said, "Maybe you could tell me where the pawnshops are in this town."

Living Simply is the Best Revenge

Tallahassee, Florida

The notes and the sketches are still there, in a warped manila folder marked THE HOUSE, and when it is late at night and I am warm from wine and the fireplace in our apartment I will take out the file and do my dreaming. The sounds of cops and street urchins and fire engines and city dogs are wailing through the windows. The dream is to build my own two-story cabin in the far northeast corner of Georgia, up there where they filmed James Dickey's *Deliverance*, but the dream transcends geography. The dream is all about finding a way to get even with the bastards who issue credit cards and build disposable cars and design throwaway clothes and convince you of the need for dishwashers and electric can openers and haircuts and television sets and canned soup and shaving cream and toothpaste and electric blankets and frozen foods and country-club memberships and "legal advice" and "preventive dental care" and a million other things that would make Henry David Thoreau retch if he came back tomorrow. I invite the following professionials and experts not to call me until I call them—lawyers, dietitians, mechanics, house painters, veterinarians, plumbers, welcome-wagon ladies, electricians, psychoanalysts, and carpenters (there are many more)—because I can do very well without them with what

I have learned in forty-odd years on God's Green Earth.

I am not being frivolous about this. For fourteen years I was married to a woman who was born on the eve of Pearl Harbor, who slept through the rationing and belt-tightening and night-time air-raid drills of the early forties as a baby in a cradle, and whose real life began when suddenly there were jobs and cars and clothes and new houses and all the other things that accrue to the winner of a war. She came of age during the fifties wanting every-thing Ike promised—dishwashers, side-by-side refrigerators, tail-finned Chryslers, air conditioning, television, the latest fashions, rosy-faced babies, credit cards, suburban houses, vacuum cleaners, beauty shops ("hair stylists"), cute puppy dogs, and Norman Rockwell holiday gather-round-the-table feasts—because she'd been taught that she had it coming to her.

My memories, on the other hand, were a bit more ragged. I had entered the first grade in 1942, when it looked like the Japs were going to be here before I turned seven, and to this day I can re-member how grim it all was with the rationing and the air raids and no car and those gold stars in front-room windows and living off cereal for a week. Rolling tin-foil balls and listening to FDR during his fireside chats and learning to walk if you needed to be somewhere and doing without: That is what the forties in America came to, in hopes that a better day would somehow, miraculously, arrive. How does a kid even imagine owning a car one day when to him the way to reach Point B from Point A is to stand on the curb at First Avenue in Birmingham, Alabama, and finger a dime in his pocket while waiting for a trolley?

When we married, one Saturday in 1961, inside the cavern of an edifice-complex Baptist church on the upwardly mobile side of Birmingham, the friends I had invited to be ushers were put out at me because of the extra rent they had to pay for morning pants and swallowtail coats. There was a phalanx of photographers to record it all in color and in black and white (at something like four hundred dollars). Then the reception, both of us wearing new clothes. Then the ritual honeymoon, both of us taking along more new clothes in new luggage, at a tacky mountain resort named Gatlinburg in the Tennessee Smokies. There followed, of course,

minutes and hours and days and weeks of planning the future together: white picket fences, bedroom suites, sofas, televisions,
babies, cars, Thanksgiving dinners, Christmases around the tree,
pets, roasted turkeys, and so on *ad nauseam.*

But first, a credit card. They made it so easy ("Young couple
like you, good income, steady job, sign here"). Then another credit
card. Then some furniture bought on time. Another credit card. A
new car, two hundred down and whatever it was a month for the
"growing family." Credit card. Elegant furnishings for the new
baby ("You want your child to have the best, don't you?") and a
dog for the kid to play with ("You remember seeing *Lassie, Come
Home?"*) and a new apartment every year ("First month's rent
free!!") and still more credit cards and refinanced loans and out-
of-pocket debts to friends. Any Southerner, familiar with such
Rainmakers as snake-oil and patent-medicine and aluminum-
siding salesmen, should have known better. But I found myself, at
the age of thirty-five, with three children and two mortgages and
two broken cars and a dog and a cat and twenty-five thousand
dollars in debts and a drinking problem.

There is that limbo that men go through when they have finally
made the decision to run away from a hopeless impasse—leave the
kids, abandon the house, run away from home—and the experience can be traumatic. No longer is there someone to cook your
meals and wash your socks and iron your shirts and answer the
phone. You are out there alone, for the first time since your
mother stopped doing those things for you, and it is like having a
case of the bends. You have to make a reentry. "When I was divorced and going through the same thing from the other end," a
woman friend of mine recently said, "I always knew what to look
for when I dropped by some guy's apartment. I looked for how
high the clothes were piled in the corner and how many dirty
dishes were in the sink. There's a certain smell in a man's apartment that tells you he isn't ready. He hasn't learned to take care of
himself." Hasn't learned to take care of himself. It is a hell of a
burden to one who has been taken care of for the first forty years
of his life. My teenage daughter may never forget how I tried to

stretch some vegetable oil with water in order to' fry some potatoes.

The precise moment all of this came to me is still clear. I was
living in an eighty-five-dollar-a-month basement apartment (utilities included) in a suburb of Tallahassee, Florida, frenetically
banging out a magazine article and worrying about my ex-wife's
calling the sheriff at the same time, when there was a rap on the
door. It was a bony young blonde I had once known, only vaguely,
and she wore a backpack. She was hitchhiking from California to
Georgia and wondered if she could stay a few days. This lady,
about thirty, had taken care of herself her entire life. One day
during her stay she took a look at my aging, scarred tomcat—Stud
Cantrell, named after the hero of the novel I was writing—and
said, "Stud's got worms."

"Worms?"

"You can tell by the white in his eyes."

"Worms." I saw a fifteen-dollar vet bill flash.

"You got any garlic around this place?"

I had some garlic. She took a knife from her backpack and cut
out a quarter of a clove. "Come here, Stud," she yelped, sneaking
up on him from behind and putting a vise hold on his neck so he
couldn't move his jawbone either way. She slammed the chunk of
garlic down his throat, and he never had an option about swallowing it. "He's gonna smell like hell for a couple of days," she
said. But by the next day Stud Cantrell had the purest stool in
Tallahassee.

When she left I became Felix Unger, of *The Odd Couple.* Every
Monday morning I whipped up a vat of homemade vegetable
soup. I painted up the place. I unplugged my television set. I
patched up some torn shirts. I painted the El Cheapo "student's
desk" my landlady had granted me with two coats of high-gloss
black enamel. I hung some drapes and cleaned the windows and
stained the bookcases and whitewashed the walls and warned
Stud Cantrell about what was in it for him if he kept messing
around in the dirt. I learned how to take care of myself without
the help of vets and painters and decorators and dietitians and

McDonald's and analysts in a single month after my friend's visit. The last I heard of Teri Foster she was living in a commune in rural Delaware. She taught me how to live when she shoved a hunk of garlic down my sick cat's throat. She is a friend of mine.

So. What we have here is a forty-one-year-old who has, as a friend once put it, "seen the elephant and heard the owl." I know what it is like to be broke, and I know the cold-sweat feeling of hearing those reasonable voices in the night: the TV pitchman hawking one toothpaste over another, the lawyers saying one should not wander off into that dark night without "representation" (you should hear about the job my attorney did for my ex-wife in the divorce), the electricians warning about amateurs' putting bulbs into sockets, the automobile mechanics speaking in ponderous tones about how only a "licensed mechanic" truly understands the vagaries of dumping a quart of oil into a crankcase.

I don't need any of these people. My mother taught me that a healthy meal is composed of something red (meat) and something green (beans, peas, lettuce, broccoli, asparagus) and something white (potatoes, corn, rice) and something wet (water, tea) and something sweet (pie, ice cream, watermelon). My old man taught me that anybody with any sense can place Part A into Part B. Richard Nixon showed me everything I care to know about lawyers. Teri Foster taught me how to take care of my animals. I learned on my own that the packaged term Transcendental Meditation really stands for Afternoon Nap. Anybody with a ruler and the ability to chew gum and walk at the same time can frame and wall and insulate and roof and wallpaper and paint and heat and electrify a house.

The dream, then, is to get shod of these people. I want me a vegetable garden. I want to keep my money stuffed under my mattress. I want to raise my own chickens and pigs and cows. I want a kerosene lamp. I want to get my water from a well. I want a fireplace and a watermelon patch and my books and some neighbors and the woman who is so good to me and my children and a homemade-ice-cream maker and a front-porch swing and a shiny new copper kettle to cook vegetable soup in. What we need, these days, is a clean, well-lighted place that doesn't have to be bought on credit.

Runaway, Age 40

Birmingham, Alabama

Well I'm goin' to California
  Where they sleep out every night.
I'm leavin' you, woman,
  'Cause you don't treat me right.

Jimmie Rodgers, "California Blues"

There was no reason to expect things to be any different. I hadn't experienced eight straight hours' sleep for nearly two years. So why shouldn't I be up at six o'clock on a Sunday morning, watching Oral Roberts on a motel color television set? I was drinking warm Scotch from a tumbler and scratching my groin and watching the World Action Singers warble about somebody they call Jesus, lazing my eyes now and then toward the two children asleep on one of the beds in the room, and I kept trying to remember exactly how John Steinbeck put it about the frogs in *Cannery Row*. This was after Mack and the Boys had terrorized the population of a pond north of Monterey in what every Steinbeck freak calls the "Great Frog Hunt"—they had thrashed and clattered through a waist-deep pond and gathered nearly a thousand frogs like so many berries—and it had been only the truly terrified frogs that had managed to escape. "Those," Steinbeck wrote, "decided to leave this place forever to find a new world where this sort of thing didn't happen."

That was precisely what I was doing. At the age of forty I was running away from home. A fourteen-year marriage had blown up in my hands. In the wake were three fatherless children and ten thousand dollars in debts and a drinking problem and an embittered ex-wife whose vindictiveness bordered on the indecent (she had taken to calling me only hours before I was to make a long drive to pick up the children, to say I couldn't see them until I "paid every cent" I owed her). For two years I had treated my typewriter like bad water—circling it and thirsting for it but unable to summon the courage to use it—and had run to the comfort of a part-time university teaching job where I more or less taught remedial spelling to a bunch of black kids who didn't really care whether the sun came up.

Molly, the four-year-old, awoke first in the motel room. Cherubic, blond, precocious, she was the best and the brightest of the three. "Daddy," she said, still wiping the sleep from her eyes, "do you like Grandmother?"

"My mother? Sure."

"I mean Mama's mother."

"No, honey, I don't think so."

"Why?"

"She's mad because I left. She does bad things to me."

"Well," Molly said, and shrugged. "She told me she hates you."

Oh, my God, I thought, *what happened? What the hell's going on around here?* Except for brief adventures in France and New England I had spent my entire life in the South. I was the son of an Alabama truck driver and had always lived under the shadow of an ethic that says the perseverant shall inherit the earth. I was taught that if I worked hard and was honest to my neighbors, all of the right things would happen: a white two-story frame house in a quiet neighborhood, retirement benefits, a savings account, model children, new car every other year, no discernible sweat. But when they told me that, I thought as I kissed the children and turned my car west toward Memphis and Denver and San Francisco on a quixotic three-thousand-mile hunt for a new life, they neglected to tell me about the devils who would be hiding behind bushes and now and then flinging obstacles in my way. Woman abruptly resents man. Man reacts by hating woman. Woman poisons children. Man leaves. Woman hires lawyer. Man drinks. Children cry. Man knows he needs fresh start in new town.

And so I pondered California. California is where you go to forget. Go west, old man, and become new and whole again. California is the ultimate fresh start. California, Steinbeck had further told me, is where you pick oranges from trees when you are hungry and sleep out every night when you are tired and do what you jolly well please when you are bored. So I cut and ran, going against everything my old man had ever told me about the importance of being rooted, and when I reached California a week later I began to wonder if maybe we don't take our baggage with us no matter where we try to hide.

"Tell me about California," I said to a new friend when I had settled into San Francisco. He was an old photographer who knew the city well. He had been with *Life* magazine for years and had photographed more movie starlets in his time than he cared to think about, and now he was lunching after having presided over an exhibit of his photographs downtown.

"It's the jumping-off point," he said.

"How's that?"

"Literally. I mean it literally."

"Jumping-off point. The bridge?"

He said, "The Golden Gate is symbolism too good to be true. Everybody comes out here to get away from something. To start over again. Things didn't work out at the other place, wherever it was, so they come here to try it one more time. And if it doesn't work here, if they can't find the answer in San Francisco, they go to the bridge. You can't run any farther west than that."

The Coast

~~~~~~

The three men I admire most,
The Father, Son, and the Holy Ghost,
They took the last train for the Coast
The day the music died.
Don MacLean, "American Pie"

*G*reat Godawmitey. It is three thousand miles from Atlanta to San Francisco, and my bride-to-be and I have the audacity to try it in a little bitty Datsun. We are Southerners—I from Birmingham, she from a quiet suburb of Atlanta—and here we are. Headed for Out There. Memphis, Little Rock, the Ozarks, Missouri, Kansas, Colorado, Utah, Nevada. Prairie dogs, slot machines, wheat fields, corn, livestock yards you can smell ten miles away. "I want to see some kudzu," she pretends to pout somewhere around Garden City, Kansas, where the In Cold Blood killings took place. For as far as you can see there is nothing but the wheat that America is feeding Russia.

I am thinking about my old man much of this time. I wonder how many times he had seen this country while I was a kid. How many times did he stop to help somebody broken down on these Nevada highways beside a sign saying NEXT SERVICES 57 MILES? How many times did he simply pull off the road and sleep behind the wheel when he knew it was 118 miles to Albuquerque and not a motel in sight? How many snakes did he run over just because there wasn't anything better to do?

And then, finally, there was San Francisco. The Bay. Maybe the most sparkling city in the world. Looks like a toy city, all laid out there around that bay with its blue water and Alcatraz and the brown hills of Marin as a backdrop. Coming into that place after the horrors of the Deep West is an *unspeakable pleasure. So why, for a pair of Southerners, is there a dark cloud up there? What, in these most pleasurable surroundings, is so wrong? We would marry, we would have a baby, we would live in a wonderful apartment near downtown, we would have solid jobs, and we would be surrounded by friends. What's wrong? I'll tell you what is wrong with California for a Southerner.*

Californians have the following: Mercedes Benzes, plastic Christmas trees, Astroturf for lawns, Rev. Jim Jones and Werner Erhard and "space" and Governor Brown (you will not recall this name if you tune in late). Californians like to talk about their Mercedeses and their plastic Christmas trees and their Astroturf lawns and their political heroes. Californians do not like to talk about anything except California.

Tales of the City

San Francisco

He sat at one of the tables against the wall, and he faced the door so he could see the people as they came in. The place was crowded now. It was five-thirty in the afternoon, and everybody was getting off work and dropping by for a drink before fighting the traffic home. Everybody looked young and successful. He wore a dark-blue three-piece business suit, and he looked young and successful, like all the others.

He had been there for ten minutes and was having a drink when he saw her stop at the door and look for him through the semidarkness. She was young and very pretty. When he stood up she saw him and walked quickly to his table. He circled around the table and helped her into her chair. She left her coat on. He sat back down across the table from her.

"I was about to give up," he said.

"What time is it?" she asked him.

He looked at his watch. "Five-thirty-five," he said.

"I'm just five minutes late."

"One minute, I panic."

"I had to run by the post office."

"It's all right," he said. "I just got here anyway."

A waitress came over and placed a paper napkin on the table in front of her and asked what she would like to drink. She told her a glass of Chablis. He told the waitress he would have another Scotch on the rocks. When the waitress had gone, they sat in silence and looked at each other.

"You look tired," he said after two or three minutes.

"There was a lot of typing at the last minute."

"Is that it?"

She looked up at him, abruptly. "What?"

"You're tired? There was a lot of work?"

"What are you getting at?"

"Forget it," he said. He tore a corner from his napkin.

"No. Really. What did you mean?"

"You sounded different on the phone. Afraid. I don't know. You still want to go through with it, don't you?"

"You got a cigarette?" she said.

He gave her a Marlboro and lighted it for her. The waitress brought their drinks. They did not speak until the waitress had left again. It gave her time to think.

"Well?" he said.

"I'm not sure."

"I thought we'd gone over this."

"It's not easy."

"Does he suspect anything?"

"Yes, I think. I'm not sure."

"The plans are made. It's all set."

"It's easier for you," she said. "There's nobody else involved with you. What is it you say? 'Remain a moving target.' No kids, no house, none of that. Me, I'm running out of excuses. All he has to do is call one of those 'girlfriends' I'm always going out to lunch with and it's all over. He'll know."

He bolted down his drink, then lit a cigarette for himself. They both knew it was beginning to sound like a soap opera, like something out of Arminstead Maupin's "Tales of the City" in the *Chronicle*. "You're being very adult all of a sudden."

"A mother *is* an adult," she said.

"You're right. You're absolutely right."

"Don't say it like that."

"How *do* I say it? We go along like this for months, then you suddenly remember you're married. You want me to forget it ever happened, I guess."

She said, "I don't know. I just don't know. I've tried to think it out, but I can't. I just don't know."

He squinted through the windows, where the late-afternoon sun was beginning to glare. "Another drink?" he said.

"No," she said. "He's coming home tonight from Chicago. I've got to relieve the maid. Bobby's feeling bad. There's a bug, I think. The baby's sick. Oh, Christ. No. I've got to leave. Christ."

"Can I walk you to the car?"

"You'd better not."

"The weekend's open. I'll call you tomorrow."

"All right. He'll be there, but all right."

She got up quickly and walked out the door, and he watched as the light from outside fell on her hair and shoulders. Then she was gone. He adjusted his eyes to the dark bar again.

"Another?" the waitress asked.

"Yes," he said. "I guess so."

Starting Over

San Francisco

Because my life seems to feed off impulses rather than cool logic, it came as no surprise when I found myself looking up from the absolute bottom of the mine one Halloween. This was around 1974, getting toward midnight in a Laundromat on the seedy fringes of downtown Montgomery. Much earlier that day I had left a note for my wife of fourteen years and slammed some books and clothes into a two-hundred dollar junker station wagon and said farewell to my first life. Now, at an hour when Lisa and David and Molly would be out terrorizing the citizens of our little island on the coast of Georgia, I found myself watching my clothes dry in the presence of a hunched-over old black man, four hundred miles to the west.

"You ain't out spookin' tonight?" he said, wearily smiling after reading the *Montgomery Advertiser* one more time. He sat next to the wide plate-glass window in hopes of catching a neighborhood kid soaping obscenities in the window.

"Did that this morning," I told him.

"Morning? Spookin' this morning?"

"Ran away from home. Scared my kids."

The old man blinked. What he saw was a forty-year-old man

with a load of clothes spinning in the dryer, and the man was telling him he had already celebrated Halloween by frightening his
own children. "Ran away from home, you say," the old man said.

"This morning. Yes, sir."

"No costume, nothin' like that? For Halloween?"

"Pair of jeans, boots, T-shirt."

"Humph." The old man snapped open the *Advertiser*. "See what
the gov'nor had to say yesterday?"

You cry. God knows, you cry, and you curse the dream you had
of a picket-fenced house and a shiny Chevrolet and a lush green
front yard and a Sears swing set in the backyard and three or four
children to call you Daddy. You were programmed to believe that
if you studied and stayed out of what they called "trouble" and
minded your manners and went to church, you were entitled to all
of these things. More important, you were convinced that these
things were worth having. Ike was president. The Korean War
was over. Music was provided by Elvis Presley and Patti Page,
scenery by Robert Young and Fred MacMurray and Doris Day,
and you were given no hints that Hollywood was presenting anything less than a true picture of marriage.

So we went into it, we products of the fifties, with every promise
that all of it was right. I was a very young twenty-five, she a very
young twenty, when I proposed (on my knees, of course, while she
sat on the sofa in a dress that told me she knew this was the day it
would happen). I had been accepted for a new job in a new line of
work. She said yes, we kissed passionately, the phone rang, I said
yes to the job, we sketched out our new life, and her mother began
preparing for the wedding. Now I look back and see how fervently
we wanted to hang on to the memory of that time and believe it
could blot out the rest.

We simply grew apart. Three children couldn't keep it together.
I went one way, she another, and the kids got caught in the middle. It was a foolish way to marry. Not only did we not know each
other; we didn't know ourselves. Neither party should be blamed.
You blame the American Dream—the one being perpetuated

then by Fred Astaire and all of those sappy pop singers and shel-
lacked movie stars—but you don't blame the principals. We were
only doing what, in our time, came naturally.

On a Saturday morning some two years after my divorce I was
kicked awake by the woman who would, that very afternoon, become the second Mrs. Paul Hemphill. We had been together for
nearly a year. Her first marriage had gone much like mine, except
that there were no children involved in hers, and now we found
that if we didn't know what we wanted, at least we knew what we
didn't want. She and I had been sharing things—an apartment,
underarm deodorant, bed, comb, TV, books, car—for three
months. It was a fine old apartment building overlooking the Bay,
loaded with saucy old blue-haired dowagers ("Well," they would
invariably prod the resident manager as he ferried them up the
elevator shaft, "have they married *yet?*"), and it was in that apartment building, so far away from what we Southerners knew as
home, that we learned to know each other and ourselves. But now
I was being kicked awake at dawn, on my second wedding day, by
the bride-to-be. "Okay, Hemphill," she said, "your ninety-day
free-home-demonstration period is up. Either pay up or return the
merchandise." So we went off to get married.

We had found ourselves humming that sappiest of sappy wedding songs, "The Second Time Around," but with fervor, as we
went through the details of getting blood tests and securing a license and arranging for the ceremony. It would be held in the
backyard of *San Francisco Examiner* sports columnist Wells Twom-
bly and his wife, Peggy, officiated by a Carolina-born rabbi-
turned–Superior Court judge, attended by fifty-odd friends at
poolside in the calm of a northern California suburban town.
Hemphill even bought a velvet coat to go with his faded jeans and
halfway promised to wear a tie. Susan—Susan Farran Percy,
thirty-two, Phi Beta Kappa, reporter—bought a special suit.
There would be dinner and an obligatory "wedding night" in
Monterey.

Of course we would refer to it as the Wedding of the Year.
Enough whiskey to float the aircraft carrier *Coral Sea.* Photogra-

phers everywhere, naturally, when the principals are journalists. A veteran three-year-old ring bearer. A sometime rabbi marrying a redneck atheist and a backsliding Catholic, all three from the south, before fifty cynical journalists at poolside in California is what Herb Caen, the columnist, would call an "item." Wedding cake topped by the Twomblys' original bride-and-groom statue. Men taking their billfolds out of their pockets in case an impromptu swimming orgy might ensue. Happy tears, at the end, when the history of the rings was revealed: The groom's belonged to her late father; it was a silver, cowboyish ring made thirty-five years earlier on Fifth Avenue in New York. The bride's was part of the loot involved when his parents were married for free in a "Perfect Couple" wedding on the stage of a movie house in Birmingham during the Depression. And off they went, these by-products of the fifties trying to forget the Dream and to start over as adults; off they went to see if there really is a second life after a first death.

"The wedding announcement," she said as she picked the grains of rice from her hair and shoes and cleavage (there had been no rice that season in northern California) and the car sped southward toward Steinbeck Country.

"Wedding announcement," he said.

"I want my picture in the paper. 'New Bride.' "

"It'd be embarrassing."

"Embarrassing. What do you mean by that?"

"They can't say 'The bride wore white.' "

"Well," she said, "at least they can give our address."

"Address? I don't want people knowing our address."

"Something like, 'Following the ceremony the couple will be at home. Where they have been for the past ninety days.' "

The Grapes of Wrath

San Francisco

There was only one way for John Steinbeck's novel to end. The Joad family, reaching the end of the rope in California, stumble into a barn during a fierce rainstorm. Rose of Sharon, the daughter, has just gone through a stillbirth, and her breasts are still swollen with milk. They find a boy, wide-eyed, hovering over his starving father. The matriarch of the family chases the others away and leaves Rose of Sharon with the man. "Then slowly she lay down beside him," Steinbeck wrote. "He shook his head slowly from side to side. Rose of Sharon loosened one side of the blanket and bared her breast. 'You got to,' she said. She squirmed closer and pulled his head close. 'There!' she said. 'There.' Her hand moved behind his head and supported it. Her fingers moved gently in his hair. She looked up and across the barn, and her lips came together and smiled mysteriously."

And still they come. Early yesterday afternoon a dusty Greyhound bus rolled into the station at Market Street and the tired load of humanity spilled out. There were young servicemen and Chicanos and commuters, groggy from the undulation of the bus over many miles, and there was also Faye and Don Tompkins and their three-year-old son.

"I'm going to get Robbie some soup," Faye told her husband.

"Okay."

"You want to eat?"

"I could use a beer," he said.

She pouted. "Can we afford a beer?"

"After two thousand miles, I don't give a damn."

Faye Tompkins, holding her son by the hand, walked off to the diner in the Greyhound station. Don Tompkins went off in search of a beer. Country music was playing on a jukebox. There was the pinging of pinball machines in the muggy depot. Other travelers, coming and going, stomped out cigarette butts and slept and read paperback novels while waiting to move on.

This is the movingest country in the world, and most of the roads still point to California, which is supposed to be where a man can live off oranges and soak up the sun and bump into a movie star on the street now and then. Some notions never die. John Steinbeck wrote about it in *The Grapes of Wrath* nearly forty years ago ("Maybe we can start again, in the new rich land—in California, where the fruit grows. We'll start over"), and Jimmie Rodgers was singing about it even before that ("Well I'm goin' to California where they sleep out every night . . ."). It is, of course, a case of the grass's always looking greener on the other side. Geography doesn't remove problems. A fresh start in a new town seldom changes things. We take our problems, along with our underwear and shoes, with us.

Six months ago Don and Faye Tompkins knew they would be moving soon. They were childhood sweethearts in the flat country between Little Rock and Memphis. They married five years ago, when he was thirty and she was twenty-five, and when Robbie was born two years later they moved to the edge of Little Rock, where Faye stayed home to look after the baby and Don worked in a small plant where cardboard boxes were made. He was earning $5 an hour. With overtime that sometimes meant as much as $250 a week. But with inflation being what it was, and rent, medical bills, groceries, gas, that wasn't enough. Don had heard that California had plenty of jobs and that the Bay Area was a pleasant place to live, so they more or less winged it. They sold what furniture they owned, paying off their bills and buying bus tickets with the proceeds, and headed for San Francisco.

"It cost damned near two hundred fifty dollars," Don Tompkins was saying. He sat at the bar in a joint near the Greyhound station. They had spent nearly a week on the road. The kid had taken a cold from the air conditioning on the trip. Don had deep rings under his eyes, and his clothes were wrinkled, and when he talked he turned his face so nobody would smell his breath.

"What?" he was asked. "The fare? It's two hundred fifty dollars?"

"Then we had food and stuff."

"Where will you stay?"

"I've got to get Robbie to a bed. I don't know."

He said that in the beginning he would try to get work as a mechanic. He always did his own car repairs, he said. If there was one thing he knew, it was how to find out what was wrong with a car and how to fix it. He never read *The Grapes of Wrath,* he said. He never even finished high school. How was he supposed to know about how the Okies and the Arkies and the other poor Southerners had bailed out and come to California forty years ago to find a new life? "Christ," he said, "I'm just looking for a place for me and my wife and kid to sleep tonight. I don't need any crap about a book right now. I need a good hotel. Not too good, not too bad. I need a good, cheap hotel room for the night. Maybe you got a copy of that book you could send me when we kind of get settled in somewhere."

Jerry U-Haul

San Francisco

Jerry U-Haul got his nickname when he became known in certain circles as the fastest mover in the world. One time, when he was living in a four-dollar-a-day room in Queens, Jerry managed to relocate to another hotel in twenty-three minutes flat. This record can be verified by the dozen or so people who were standing outside the neighborhood bar with draft beers in hand, cheering, as Jerry crossed the wires on a panel truck parked at the curb and borrowed the truck long enough for the one trip required to move all of his worldly possessions. Jerry left a five-dollar bill on the front seat, with a note of profuse thanks. "I always look out for the Little Guy," he explains. That made eight moves for Jerry in that particular year.

All of this moving has been necessary because Jerry U-Haul is big on credit and the people who issue credit are always wanting their money back. The other day, from his latest address on Mission Street, Jerry was beaming over a letter he had just written to a loan shark. The loan shark had threatened to do dangerous things to Jerry if Jerry didn't pay back the thousand dollars he had borrowed to visit a dying sister in Lake Tahoe. The letter read,

Gentlemen.

Each month I write the names of my creditors on slips of paper and place the slips in a hat. I then draw from the hat and send checks to the lucky winners. Apparently, your name was not drawn from the hat last month. Now you send me a dirty letter. Just for that I am not going to put your name in the hat next month.

Jerry U-Haul was so pleased with himself that he went out that afternoon and bought a $315 color television set on time. "Time," he said as the Monday Night Movie flashed on in brilliant color that evening in his room. "All I need is time. By the time the first payment is due, I'll be in Kansas City."

This ability to go one up on the usurers, in this day and in this time, has virtually made a folk hero out of Jerry U-Haul. They like to talk about "tight money" these days, but you would never know it by the way the banks and oil companies and various credit companies send out credit cards all over the country. One time I tried to give Hertz two hundred dollars up front to rent a car for Christmas afternoon in Norfolk, Virginia, and I had to give them the name of the magazine editor I was working for so he could verify I wasn't crazy because I didn't use charge cards. Cash doesn't work anymore.

Jerry U-Haul learned this a long time ago. "Look," he was saying last week, "they're asking for it. If somebody leaves the keys in the car and a full tank of gas and a map of North America, what am I gonna do? Right? So if these jerks are dumb enough to send me a credit card or lend me money otherwise, I'll take it." Jerry fills out application forms every chance he gets. He has charge cards in twenty different names. The addresses he has used make him sound like Magellan. He normally gives a nice round figure of seventy thousand as his annual income and lists important banks as references, and no matter what name he uses he always begins it the same way. "From my experience," Jerry says, "no man ever amounted to much unless his name began with the initial 'J.' J. Paul Getty. J. Pierpoint Morgan. You can look it up."

Once the card or the money is in hand, the rest is easy. Jerry U-

Haul simply runs low and often. This trust of credit cards runs so deep that all you have to do is fumble through your billfold in search of the proper card, flashing card after card for the benefit of an astounded salesman, and they will give you anything. "Yes, *sir,* Mr., ah, Mr. J. Grove Whitman, I see, and could we interest you in a new sofa today?" they say to Jerry while he is charging a marble-topped coffee table, spilling credit cards all over like confetti.

The only time there is trouble is when, somehow, they find out where Jerry U-Haul is living at the moment. Almost always he leaves a forwarding for somewhere like Salina, Kansas, or Keene, New Hampshire, with the post office, but now and then he leaves a trace and the creditors come swarming as though he were the Dalton Gang and they the FBI. "What you got to do then is intimidate the bastards," says Jerry. "Do it to them before they do it to you."

Two years ago Jerry owed seventeen hundred dollars to a national credit card company, and one night at ten o'clock the phone rang while a half dozen of Jerry's closest friends were splitting two gallons of Wild Irish Rose wine. Some college kid moonlighting with a collection agency was calling from New York and wanting to know about the seventeen hundred.

"What's your name, kid?" Jerry shouted into the phone.

"But, sir, I don't see what that has to—"

"By God, kid, you know *my* name. What's *yours?*"

The kid gave his name. "We very seriously want to know, Mr., ah, Mr. Smith, exactly when you propose to—"

"Is that your real name, kid?"

"I beg your pardon. There's no reason to get personal."

"Get *personal,*" Jerry shrieked. "Listen to the jerk, who calls me when I'm already asleep. *Personal.* Hey, kid. Does your mother know what you do for a living?"

With that, Jerry U-Haul hung up and stalked back to his friends in the living room. They gave him a standing ovation. He never heard from the company again.

John Dillinger, Jr.

San Francisco

T ennessee gets out of the county jail in about a
week now, and the people down at the sheriff's
department are figuring this is one kid they will never see again. His
real name is Tom Wilkins. He is twenty-three, single, a lanky,
drawling fellow who was born in Memphis and acts like it. Everybody likes him out at San Bruno, where he has been in jail for
nearly a year. He does whatever odd jobs need doing, and in the
late afternoon he sits out on the front steps of the jail up in the hills
there and smokes cigarettes and ticks off the minutes and the
hours until his release. He thinks he will enroll in a printing school
next month, after his release. "You're looking at the worst bank
robber the world ever produced," one of the jailers was saying the
other day. Tennessee stroked his faint mustache and blushed.

The only other trouble Tennessee ever had with the authorities
was when he got an undesirable discharge from the U.S. Marine
Corps for possession of marijuana. He was never cut out to be a
bad guy. He grew up all right. He quit before he finished high
school in Memphis, to join the Marines, and maybe that was part
of his problem. But he liked the normal things, like beer and girls
and messing around. Nobody back home would have thought he

would wind up trying to play John Dillinger, Jr., in San Francisco, California.

The trouble started more than a year ago when Tennessee rode a motorbike all the way here from Memphis. He didn't have any firm idea of what he would do in the city. It just sounded like a good place. So he came here without any skills and started sleeping at friends' and looking for a job. The money was running low. He had to sell his bike. He washed dishes and changed tires and parked cars. He made new friends.

One of Tennessee's new friends said he knew a sure way to make some money. This friend, Joe, had an uncle who made a large deposit every day at a Bank of America branch downtown. For two weeks they hung out near the bank and got the uncle's schedule down pat as he walked to the bank with a white canvas sack and made his afternoon deposit. When the police went on strike last August, Tennessee borrowed a gun from a friend, and he and Joe motored over from the Tenderloin to make some money.

At three P.M. they were parked in front of the bank. Joe cranked the engine of his car. Tennessee, with the gun in his pocket, got out of the car and said he would be right back. "This won't take a minute," he said. Then he walked up to the distinguished façade of the bank and leaned against it and lit a cigarette as though he were waiting for a friend. Like clockwork, the uncle came down the sidewalk within two minutes. Her was carrying the white sack and merely running an errand, as usual, except this time there was fourteen thousand dollars in the sack.

"Pardon me, sir," Tennessee said when the uncle reached the wide doors to the bank.

"Yes?" The uncle didn't seem to be worried. He didn't know whom he was confronting here.

"Which way is, ah, which way is Bayshore?"

"Bayshore? Oh, well, you go three blocks—"

"What's in the bag?"

"—three blocks, and then— Hey."

Tennessee flashed the .44-caliber Magnum and told the uncle he wanted the sack. The uncle, still cool, asked Tennessee what he wanted the sack for. Tennessee said he wanted the sack because there was a lot of money in it. The uncle said he was sorry, but he didn't want anybody to have the sack unless it was the bank. Tennessee cocked the pistol and looked mean, and the uncle gave him the sack of money.

Everything was going right on schedule. Nobody in the bank had seen anything. The street was clear of cops. Tennessee grabbed the sack and spun away, expecting Joe to have the door open and the motor running, but he saw the car screeching away from the curb. The uncle was shouting, "Joe. What the hell. Joe." For Tennessee there was only one option. He shoved the gun in his pocket and began to walk down the sidewalk, away from the bank. He walked very fast.

The uncle threw open the doors to the bank and said he had just been robbed of fourteen thousand dollars, and a covey of bank officials came running behind him. They caught up with Tennessee and told him he had done a bad thing and could they have the money back. None of this was supposed to have happened. Usually the getaway car is waiting when they do it on television. Tennessee was doing a lot of heavy thinking.

"The money, son. Give us the sack."

"Sure," Tennessee said. "You want the gun, too?"

"The money and the gun," said the bank official.

"I wasn't gonna use it anyway. I was just playing."

One of the bank people said he could understand how a young desperate kid might make such a mistake. He said that since they had the money there really hadn't been a robbery after all and recommended that Tennessee go down to the corner and catch a bus. He even told Tennessee which bus to catch. Tennessee jammed his hands in his pockets and whistled off toward the bus stop, and he felt relieved about everything right up to the minute he got a ride in the squad car.

Whiskey

San Francisco

They met thirteen years ago in San Francisco, and within six weeks they were engaged to marry. He was a cop, Spanish, more or less the breadwinner for a sprawling family. She was a lovable woman, thirty, eager to have a large family of her own. So they married, and she promptly began to have babies. She had six of them, roughly one per year for the first seven years of their marriage, and stayed at home mothering them while he went about his business of becoming as good a cop as he could become. It wasn't easy for her, being the wife of a dedicated cop, but she endured it because he was good and she believed in him. "We had," she says even today, after what happened, "a lovely marriage."

He was right out of one of those television series. For seventeen years everything he did and thought was keyed to police work. He would sneak around in the shank of the night, in plainclothes, making arrests on his own time. He wound up on television and radio shows, talking about undercover police work. Born and reared in San Francisco, he had managed only to finish high school, but he was one of those people who wanted to be either a cop or a concert pianist. There would be none of this sitting behind a desk or selling insurance or driving a truck for him. He had presence. He wanted to leave a mark. He was a *visible* man, and his kids and his wife loved him for that.

The trouble began some six years ago when he got involved in a kidnap case, perhaps too vigorously, and went under investigation by the police department. He took a leave of absence and went into a used-car business with his sister. The business lost money, and that compounded his troubles, and he began to drink. Until then a couple of cocktails at the end of the day had been his limit, and he would always keep asking people if he seemed to be drunk and was always apologizing for "drinking so much." But now the drinking became destructive. Last November he quit the police department for good and took disability for his ulcers. He went home, alone and out of work, with six kids and a wife to feed, and he stared at his breakfast and began hitting the bottle by eleven o'clock in the morning.

He went into the upholstery business, setting up a shop in his garage, but that merely left him at home, where he was close to his liquor cabinet. She didn't know anything about alcoholism then. "You'll get hooked on that stuff," she would say to him. "Nah, not me. I know how to handle it," he would say. The upholstery business was slow getting started, and the bills began to stack up. He became a tortured man. He had wanted to do great things, but now he found himself a forty-eight-year-old failure. By noon he was drunk and cursing. When one of the kids opened a candy bar, with all of that rustling of paper, he would go berserk. She knew then that it was only a matter of time.

A month ago he left them, paying two months' rent on their house near Daly City and leaving her twenty dollars in cash. He moved in with his brother, but the brother and his wife were doing so much drinking and fighting that he couldn't take it, and so he moved in with an old friend from his days as a cop. Meanwhile, she was in a bad fix. She was still attending Alanon meetings, for the families of alcoholics, but she was filing for divorce. Her rent is $350 a month, and there are the six kids to take care of. She is getting help from the St. Vincent de Paul Society, but the utilities keep getting turned off, and it will be a scramble until she gets onto full welfare. She is suing him for $650 a month in child support (his disability from the police department comes to $630 a month) and hoping for $534 a month in welfare and $74 a month in food stamps.

With all of that going on, she showed remarkable poise and perspective the other night after she had the children to bed and began talking about it. She had a fierce urge to talk about alcoholism and about the welfare system. "I can't believe that the mind of this person was so great until alcohol took over," she was saying. "When he left he said, 'Take care of them,' and I said, 'With what?' A woman at the alcoholic center said the sooner he lands in jail, the sooner he will straighten out. I just don't know. I really don't care if I live or die anymore. I'll try to talk to him about his problem and he'll just say, 'So how're all of your friends down at Alanon?' Meanwhile, the utilities are being cut off and the kids are asking about Daddy and I'm going crazy." She talked a lot about how God works in mysterious ways and even seemed to hold out hope that her husband would straighten out and they could go back together, always making it clear that he was "such a different person" before whiskey took over his life. "If you had only known my husband before," she says, stopping before she begins to cry.

The other day she was talking to the people at the welfare office. She was filling out forms. The welfare workers said she hadn't completed one form. "You have to say that you are willing to work full-time," the woman told her. "But I'm a mother and I have six children to take care of," she said to the welfare worker. "Well," she was told, "to get the money you'll have to promise you'll put the kids in a child-care center and go to work if a job comes up." She went ahead and wrote down the promise and began to pray no job came up. Then her husband called. That was last Sunday night. They talked about the kids for a while. When she found an opening she wondered aloud if he would consider calling a Catholic center for alcoholics. He hung up on her.

Sad Lady

San Francisco

S he looks like your mother. She has a clean face that
is a little pinched around the nose and mouth and
reminds you of a nun's face. Her gray hair has been carefully
gathered in a bun and stuffed under a dainty white scarf. She
wears a royal-blue sweater over a stark white blouse, and then
there is a dark-red skirt with gaudy ruffles that swish back and
forth when she walks. She walks tentatively, as if she doesn't want
to interrupt anything that might be going on, and she speaks in a
soft, sweet tone except when she talks about what other people are
trying to do to her. "One or two times," she says, "some finks
called the police about me and I had to change my territory."

That was when she was trying to sell things to make a living.
She sold all kinds of things. Once she sold coupons for a photo-
graphic studio. Another time she sold facial tissues. Other times it
was dishes, stuffed animals, vases, dolls, soap, and ladies' hosiery.
She always sold these things from door to door, flashing her sweet
little-old-lady smile and giving out her long, sad story and doing
quite well, thank you. "Then this bunch of finks got tired of me
working their neighborhood, I guess," she says, "so they called the
police. The police said there wasn't anything they could do. So
they asked me to try some other neighborhood. So I did."

It is so easy to see how everything slowly got away from her. All you have to do is go back to the beginning and look at it step by step. There are so many like this in a big city like San Francisco, and most of the stories are familiar. They think the rainbow leads to the city, where the good things are supposed to be, but they will never convince themselves that the city is good for some but hell for others.

Her parents were farmers, and her memory of her father is that he was sick all of his life. There were five sisters. One of them went as far as the eighth grade; she herself made it to the sixth; and none of the other three got that far. "Everybody else dressed for school like they were going off to some big ball or something, and I couldn't do that, so I quit." When she was fourteen she left home and went to work in a nearby town. When she was twenty-two she married a cab driver. They had a daughter. Then, she says, her husband started beating her and they divorced and she never saw him again.

That was thirty years ago. Since then, from what she can learn, her ex-husband has become a manager of a plant in Ohio and has remarried and raised another family. She has not done so well. For her it has been a constant moving from place to place, getting out of touch with her sisters and even her own daughter. She has hit New York and Ohio and Kentucky and Florida and finally, seven years ago, she found herself broke and stranded in California.

And so now you have this pathetic and bitter old woman who is near sixty years of age and lives in a downtown hotel room on the twenty-five dollars a week she earns by spending every night at the home of a young Vietnam War widow who is afraid to be alone at night. Breakfast is a part of the job, and because she spends most of her money on rent and the bus fare, she seldom eats anything the rest of the day. There are not many jobs for someone like her, and life has left her with so many scars that it is not pleasant to talk with her. She wears the bitterness on her sleeve. She has reached the point of paranoia, and the paranoia is understandable.

"I'm afraid to use the phone at the hotel," she was saying the other day. "The people where I live, they seem to hate me. I think they've bugged the phone."

"Why would they bug the phone?" she was asked.

"They want to find out about me."

"What's there to find out about you?"

"Many things," she said. "Many things. I can't tell you."

"What about your family? Can they help you?"

"Many things. I can't talk about it."

"I mean, can't your daughter help?"

"Many things. Many things."

It is almost impossible to talk with her. These are the damaged people. Lost children, siblings who won't return letters, long-ago homesteads. "My daughter won't write me. Her grandmother turned her against me." What next? "I wouldn't have the least idea. I'm trying to get out of debt and out of town, that's all. 'City by the Bay.' Huh." Bitterness is a disease. Nobody should be like this, but she is.

Born Again

San Francisco

When he graduated from college years ago, he moved out on his own, and it didn't take long for the pattern of his life to begin reading like a Greyhound bus schedule. He rode freights, picked cotton, wrote poems, sold insurance, worked carnivals, read news on the radio, edited newspaper copy, and drove trucks. Wives and children were littered all over the country. He believed in Hemingway's definition of the word "morals": anything you felt good about on the morning after. By the age of fifty-five, which is when he stumbled into San Francisco, he had developed the philosophy that to live the successful life means to live only on what money is available and to do only what you truly want to do. "My only regret," he was saying the other day, "is blowing four years in college."

His life slid into a comfortable rut. He lived alone in a rundown hotel in the Tenderloin, getting the room rent-free by running the front desk and doing odd jobs, and whenever he needed a bottle of whiskey or some new socks or something special to eat, he would mind a store or sweep a floor or wash some windows and take it out in trade. Earthy, bearded and weathered, he would have made some kid an interesting grandfather. He liked to sit around and tell stories ("Lies, all lies, but *good* lies") and have a beer and read and watch the ships dock at the waterfront and, if he got lucky enough to fall into a ticket for a game, go out and watch the Giants play baseball.

Her story was something else. She came out of a small town in Oregon, one of seven children in an isolated farm family, and had taken to prostitution before she left high school. There was a problem with fat. She did get married once, and although one of her sisters had birthed five babies, she had been unable to conceive. So she ran away from Oregon and wound up in San Francisco, where she worked the sleazier parts of town for ten and twenty dollars a shot.

When they met it was late in the morning, in a diner near his hotel in the Tenderloin. He had gone into the place for a hamburger and a beer, and while he waited for his order he lighted his corncob pipe and looked around. She was sitting on the other side of the diner, hunched over an awesome breakfast of eggs with all the trimmings, and she caught his eye. She was some thirty years younger than he but she wore too much mascara and weighed nearly 185 pounds. "I love a corncob pipe," she yelled to him across the expanse of linoleum.

"Me, too," he said.

"It's manly."

"It smokes easy."

"You want to sit with me?"

He wasn't sure what he was getting into, but he said, "Sure."

And that is how it began. His hamburger and beer came, and he and she ate while they talked, and before he knew it they were walking to a market and buying hamburger meat and beer and grapes and things. They set up housekeeping. Supplies were stored in the refrigerator. Cigarettes began being shared. His clothes lay strewn on the floor at night. Her pantyhose decorated the bathroom.

He knew what she did for a living, of course, though he tried to shut it out for a while. She would make herself absent for brief periods, and then he would get a phone call from her from a truck stop or from a strange hotel room or from the bus station. It occurred to him that on a volume basis she was prospering. He tried for a long time to live with all of that. He didn't try to change her. He tried to love her for what she was and where she came from and what she did for him. Then, inexorably, their friendship and their love and their arrangement cooled. Finally it died.

All of this took place nearly five years ago. Until a week or so ago he had not heard from her again. His life had dropped back into the same routine. He had thought of her more than once but not often enough to keep him awake at night. He had carried on—shuffling around the Tenderloin, eating alone, reading, watching, getting by—until there was a knock on his door and he opened it and there she was. She looked younger and prettier and lighter than he ever imagined she could be. She carried a briefcase.

"Well," he said.

"How *are* you?" he was asked.

"A little surprised."

"Can I come in?"

"Sure."

"Me and my friend?"

He blinked and didn't see anybody. "The Lord Jesus Christ," she said, surging through the door into the room. *Good God Almighty,* he thought, *I really pick 'em.* She sat down on his ratty bed, and they talked for a few minutes about what had happened since they had last seen each other. She had been so turned around when her mother died from drinking, she said, that she had decided it wasn't too late to change. She had found religion and a husband and a new life. They now had a child. She was back in the Bay Area, looking after her baby and going to church and caring for the child, and when she could she went out on the streets to "witness for Christ." He had an urge to talk her out of this new life. "Stay," he said. "I can't," she told him. So she left him four religious tracts and quoted Oral Roberts, and he playfully gave her some pamphlets left him one time by the Jehovah's Witnesses. That is how it ended.

The Bad Stuff

San Francisco

Out in the suburbs of Marin County the other night, over wine and spaghetti, Walt Anderson got to talking about people who don't often have wine and spaghetti. Walt Anderson is in his thirties and has the title of Director of Management and Improvement for the San Francisco County Sheriff's Department. He is a growling ex-Marine who grew up in Brooklyn alleys and played college football and, until recently, wore the last burr haircut in America. Every day Walt Anderson goes downtown in the city and writes proposals and begs for money to help the jails and sits on the parole board. This is not the kind of life Walt Anderson is accustomed to. In his previous life, the life he enjoyed the most, he hung around on the corners of the seediest neighborhoods of America and tried to help poor kids with their problems.

One of the problems, in the ghettos, is venereal disease. It is not hard to know about venereal disease if you live in the slums. The evidence of what it can do to you is everywhere. Here is one who has lost his hair. There is one who can hardly walk anymore. Here is another who is blind. You can see it everywhere, and when they get it they do not know to ask what to do about it, and so it breeds and breeds and passes from one to the other and you wonder how it will ever be checked or how it has failed to wipe out an entire neighborhood.

The social workers do the best they can. They give lectures on venereal disease, show movies and slides on it, and pass out pamphlets explaining what it is and what it looks like and how to treat it. Nobody has any way of proving how much good this does, but it is all they can do. You can try to scare the daylights out of them from time to time—show them the horrors of advanced syphilis or gonorrhea—and maybe that is the best way. "If you've got a kid who's totally ignorant about sex and VD," Anderson was saying, "scaring the hell out of him can save a lot of time."

Atlanta leads the nation in venereal disease. For several years Walt Anderson worked the streets of Atlanta, mainly in the black slums, trying to help the poor kids. One day two of them came up to him. They were about sixteen years old. One was nicknamed Dogface, the other Mustard. They looked scared.

"Hey, Walt," said Dogface. "How you tell you got something?"

"What you mean 'something'?" Anderson asked.

"Aw, you know. Sickness."

"You feel sick?"

"Aw, you know. The first time you go with a girl."

Anderson said, "Lovesickness?"

"C'mon, Walt. You know. The bad stuff."

Anderson knew. One myth in the black ghettos is that the first sexual experience, and only the first, rewards a boy with venereal disease. This has been advanced over the years by well-meaning mothers who spend a lot of time in church. The kids look at it as having to do penance. You have to pay the price, in one form or another. You don't get something for nothing. So Mustard and Dogface told Walt Anderson they had recently been introduced into manhood, under the auspices of the same young lady. It had been more than a week, and they had been expecting the sky to fall. Now, out of pure fright, they were turning to Walt Anderson for guidance.

"How do you find out, Walt?" one of them asked.

"Nothing to do but go to Memorial."

"You mean to the *hospital?*"

"It'll just take a couple of weeks. It's a good life."

Mustard said, "Man, you ain't puttin' me in no *hospital.*"

Dogface said, "I'll take my chances."

"You guys are real smart," said Anderson. "I don't blame you. Go ahead. Maybe all you'll lose will be your teeth and your eyes."

A few hours later Anderson walked into the emergency clinic with Dogface and Mustard. They were what you call reluctant. Anderson pulled one of the doctors aside and explained the situation. He said he was fairly certain there was nothing wrong with them, but maybe they should learn a lesson. The doctor, understanding the situation quite clearly from having been there before, loaded up the longest needle he could find with water and asked who was first. Mustard volunteered and marched into another room.

The doctor ordered Mustard to drop his trousers and bend over. Mustard figured that was the routine, so he went along with the gag. The doctor hit him with the needle while he was on his way down, and Mustard let out a terrifying scream and jumped off the floor. Dogface, outside waiting his turn, determined he would trust Mustard's judgment. He burst out of the waiting room, onto the street, and mixed with the wind. Anderson went running after him. A cop in the emergency entrance figured the black kid must have done something wrong, so he came running behind Anderson and Dogface. Perhaps thirty minutes later, Dogface stuck his head into the emergency clinic. He was out of breath. He said he'd thought it over a bit.

"What happens if I don't get the shot?" he said.

"Surgery," Anderson told him.

"Whatsamatter, you chicken?" asked Mustard.

Dogface gave in. He took his shot like a man. Dogface and Mustard went back to their block and told war stories the rest of the day, and they have been very cool toward strange women ever since. Call it voluntary retirement.

I'll Do the Cooking, Honey, You Pay the Rent

San Francisco

I t was bound to happen, sooner or later, and the irony was not lost on Hemphill. He had seen, in his forty-one years, a certain image grow up around him. The image was one of *macho*. His uniform consisted of faded jeans and cowboy boots and turtlenecks and pea coats and leather jackets and T-shirts painted with Coors advertisements and with female thighs opened to the sun. He smoked Camels. He drank Scotch straight from the bottle. He swam naked in frigid mountain lakes. He hung around saloons. He cussed good. His favorite impersonation was of John Wayne (*"Wall,* little lady, ya look purty good ta *maee"*). He was personal friends with Merle Haggard and Bear Bryant and James Dickey, and his favorite football team was the mean-eyed Oakland Raiders. He loved the picture a San Francisco newspaper once had run above his daily column, because it made him look like an angry young Anthony Quinn.

But now, as he stood at the picture window of his apartment overlooking San Francisco Bay, Hemphill had a problem: It was ten o'clock in the morning. He had finished washing the dishes and making the bed and dust-mopping the floors and taking out the garbage and defrosting the refrigerator and watering the plants and scooping the ashes from the fireplace and polishing the chrome in the bathroom. His bride of three months had whisked away to her newspaper job more than an hour before. He was circling his typewriter, preparing to do the next chapter in a novel about the masculine world of bush-league baseball during the fifties, but something was wrong. When he recalled what was wrong he called his wife at the office.

"Susan Percy," she said. "May I help you?"

"I'll never get used to that."

"What?"

"Christ, your name is *Hemphill* now."

"Look," she said, "I'm on deadline."

"I know. I'm sorry. I just had one question."

"Okay. But make it quick."

"What do you want for dinner? Meat loaf or chicken?"

"Whatever you say, Stud." (Using the name of the leading character in the novel, which was to be all about an aging alcoholic player-manager in Class D baseball, and she knew how much autobiography was involved.) "Just don't make it too dry."

"Dry?" Hemphill exploded. *"Dry?"*

"You know you always cook the meat too long."

"Well, suppose you come home and do the goddamn cooking."

"You forget," she said. "I pay the rent. You do the cooking. Look, I've got fifteen minutes to finish this story. Cook good. I'll see you."

Well now. What we've got is a revolution on our hands. *You do the cooking, honey, I'll pay the rent.* A few years ago a friend of mine named Mike McGrady wrote a book he called *The Kitchen Sink Papers.* It was about how he wearied of writing a daily newspaper column for *Newsday,* on Long Island, at a time when his wife, Corinne, was beginning to make big money on her own by marketing and manufacturing anything you can make (bracelets, cookbook holders, picture frames) from raw sheets of Plexiglas. So they made a deal. Mike would stay home—waking up everybody, cooking breakfast, cleaning the house, running the kids to school, preparing dinner—while Corinne, who had been having babies and cooking and playing bridge all of those years while Mike had "fun" hanging out with the boys and fighting expressway traffic and being a "star," would become the breadwinner. "We had to make a slight adjustment here," Mike told me when the arrangement had been going on for about a year. "Now I stay home for two weeks and then she takes it for two weeks. That way nobody goes crazy for more than two weeks at a time."

It isn't easy, being a househusband, especially if you were raised into manhood during the forties and fifties, when Mama was supposed to do the cooking and Daddy was supposed to pay the rent. For those of us in our forties, that was the God-given pattern. It wasn't manly, somehow, for a man to cook. Nor was it womanly for a wife to go out and fetch the bacon. A woman's place was in the home. There was this monologue from my old man back in 1954 when it was time for me to go to college and my mother had determined that the only way that would happen would be for her to take a job (at more money than he had ever made): "It just don't seem right. You and Sis got to have hot lunches and all. Got to have your clothes ironed and get to school and have your beds made. Dishes got to get washed. It's downright embarrassing, your Mama going to work. Hell, I'm the one supposed to be making the money."

And then there was this, more than twenty years later, from a young professional woman in San Francisco with one preschool child and a husband who stays home all day and wants to be an artist: "If you think he can make what I make [eighteen thousand dollars a year], you're crazy. Housekeeping drives me bananas. Anyway, what I make is all we need, and whatever he makes is gravy. He likes hanging around the house, and I like going in to work [at an advertising agency]. So what's the big deal? It's all a question of intimidation. As long as he doesn't feel intimidated by my 'paying the rent' and his 'doing the cooking,' like you put it, we got no problems."

That, essentially, is how it has been with us. We are both on our second marriage. My first was to a basic Southern housewife whose mission was to raise babies and scour pots and wipe kitchen counters and run kids to school and wait for me to come home from work. Her first was to an archaeologist who didn't want children and couldn't make much money and expected a "working wife" who would, after spending a day at the mill, come home and whip up dinner. I tried, for a while, to help out with the housework in my first wife's kitchen (it was always her kitchen) and quit when I found she was rewashing the dishes after midnight when she found my efforts lacking. Susan, my new wife, reached a point with her first husband when she determined that if he wanted peanut-butter sandwiches for dinner he could, by God, make them himself. From there, we started.

For fourteen years of marriage I made the basic assumption that clothes simply got washed and meals simply got cooked. I was busy making a living. I did the "man's work" around the various houses and apartments we occupied—wallpapering, stoking fires, sanding floors, painting, building bookcases, and all of that—but the laundering and cooking and cleaning and diapering and such were done by the mother of my three children. When I left home more than two years ago, there was much to be learned. The most shocking moment came late one night in a black ghetto of Montgomery, Alabama, when I found myself watching not television but my own clothes spinning around and around in a Laundromat.

Next came the indoctrination period. Taking care of oneself is a hell of a burden for one who has always been looked after. I had set off on a steady program of rehabilitating myself: learning how to cook basic meals, abiding the washing of clothes, rolling up the balls of dust beneath the bed, going through the discipline of making up the bed every morning. Yes. Learning how to take care of oneself is the first step toward recovery from a divorce.

You have plenty of help, of course, once word of the divorce gets around. "Poor baby," all of the matrons are saying. "We must invite Paul over for supper," they tell their husbands, "before he starves to death." You are deluged with recipes and garden tomatoes and surplus fish caught over the weekend and bell peppers grown in the backyard and spare aprons ("Thought you might need this") and potatoes found deep in the bin. Not to mention the cookbooks. My God, the cookbooks. Who the hell is this Peg

Bracken, anyway? And the surfeit of aprons continues. WHO ARE
ALL OF THESE TACKY PEOPLE? and GET OUT OF MY KITCHEN and I
BET YOU CAN'T SPELL STROODAL and WHERE'S THE COOKING
SHERRY? You want aprons. Aprons I've got.

Yes, Hemphill had problems. He found that he had abruptly
gone from breadwinner to breadmaker. Oh, for sure, there were
the little jokes. "You prove you can do that two times in a row,"
his wife would tell him after a stunning roast lamb, "and I'll personally pay for your ticket to the Pillsbury Bake-Off next year."
Free-lancing now, he found himself making do without a car and
discovering a five-dollar bill left discreetly on the bureau each
morning and jotting down phone calls left for his wife but, in general, enjoying his new role. The last thing he wanted as an epi-
taph, he decided, was to be regarded as a "good provider." There
was something condescending about being known as a "good provider." Some of his better moments would come when she would
call from the office immediately after she had left, while he was
scurrying about the place picking up everything that looked
twenty-four hours old, and ask if he had disposed of Herb Caen's
column of that morning. He felt, at those times, like a "neatnik."
There came, then, the big day of the birthday dinner. She was
turning thirty-three. The sixty-cent daisies bought down the street
wouldn't do the job. Before noon Hemphill was laboring over his
typewriter in a poem to his beloved. He did not compose a poem.
He composed a menu for a special birthday dinner—baked pork
chops and green beans and carrots and salad and a host of other
things—and he was so proud that he called friends around town to
find out how to spell these things in French so he could hoke up a
menu like they do on the plate-glass windows along Polk street.
She would be home, she said, at five-thirty.
Five-thirty came and went. It became six. It became six-fifteen.
Hemphill thought of going off to a bar somewhere, leaving a note
saying that supper was in the oven, but he thought better of it. He
put on an apron—THE PROGRESS . . . I GET IT THREE TIMES A
WEEK—and he waited. She unlocked the door to the apartment,

finally, at six-thirty. He was standing at the door, flashing his apron, with his hands on his hips. He was in a huff. "You're late," he said.

"I was on a story," she told him. "I couldn't call."

"Oh. A story. You couldn't call."

"No phones where I was."

"No phones. Where you were."

She said, "What's this? What's bugging you, ace?"

Hemphill, the former King of the Machos, slapped his hands on his hips. His hands covered his apron. He said, "What's wrong? I'll tell you what's wrong. How do you expect me to put a decent meal on the table when I never know when you'll be home?" And he saw his whole previous life flash before his very own eyes.

Georgia, Georgia

San Francisco

I t was one of the original thirteen, the southernmost of the colonies making up the charter states of the United States of America, and from the very beginning it had one foot in the grave. The bulk of its first settlers were prisoners who had been given twenty-four hours to get out of town. Georgia, when set up against Massachusetts and Pennsylvania and Virginia and the others, never was a glamorous place. All of those others had presidents and capitols and skyscrapers and international trade and fine universities and railroads and high society. Georgia, in the beginning, had gnats and swamps and slavery and grits and kudzu and pellagra and amusing little "colleges" where one could learn the fine art of plowing a straight furrow. "Thank God for Mississippi," the people of Georgia used to say not so long ago, knowing that if not for Mississippi, they would be running dead last, statistically, in everything from education to per capita income.

Even with the arrival of the 1960s, Georgia still had a bad name. This was the land of racism and demagoguery and high-school football and *Gone with the Wind* and depressing blacktop highways lined with eroding red banks of dirt and billboards proclaiming STUCKEY'S roadside joints and GEORGIA PECANS and

REAL ALLIGATORS–LIVE. To the tourists Georgia was the last place you had to endure before you made it to Florida. Ol' Eugene Talmadge and his gang of political hucksters had ruled for too long—"You got three friends in this world: Jesus Christ, Sears & Roebuck, and Eugene Talmadge"—to make Georgia an appealing place to stop.

The natives, of course, felt differently. The natives of Georgia knew a different place. They knew about the mysterious, foggy, mile-high mountains in the north. They knew about the sleepy coastal islands between Jacksonville and Savannah. They knew what was happening in Atlanta, where one third of the state's population suddenly lived, and they knew of the abrupt changes taking place in what the sociologists were calling "social relations." Georgians knew that their state had been home for such divers citizens as Lester Maddox and Martin Luther King and Otis Redding and Margaret Mitchell. It had spawned racists and populists and demagogues and bomb throwers and libertarians and libertines and sports heroes and authors and hillbilly singers and sopranos. If Georgia has been anything, it has been pluralistic.

As I write this it is a bleak Sunday afternoon in San Francisco, getting along toward dusk, some three thousand miles west of the place I have come to know as home. I moved to Atlanta twelve years ago, as a newspaper columnist, and lived there for eight years before putting in some time in a chalet in the mountains two and a half hours northwest and then spending two years living on the coastal island of St. Simons. I was in Atlanta at the time Martin Luther King was killed, when that was the only important city in America that did not suffer through race riots, and I knew the singer Otis Redding and the redneck Lester Maddox and the ballplayer Henry Aaron and the young governor Jimmy Carter. Georgians all. Black and white and liberal and conservative. Sweating, down there, and being ridiculed for being from Georgia.

It seems awfully important for me to say this because of what I have been reading lately about Jimmy Carter's ascending to the presidency. The provincialism has been overpowering. Herb Caen calls him Mistah Cahtuh, and Arthur Hoppe writes these silly things about Rosalynn and her hand-me-down dresses, and even my own boss—Reg Murphy of Gainesville, Georgia, a little mountain town, so he ought to know better—has an obsession with Carter that borders on paranoia. This northern California town, which long ago developed the notion that it was democratic, has an awful case of hate. If you aren't from San Francisco, you ain't nothing. You white trash. This is the most provincial big place (so much for Kansas and its friends) I have ever encountered.

And now, after 107 years, the Deep South has its first president. Feelings back home are, of course, mixed. On the one hand we have finally been recognized. On the other we are likely to be defiled. It is impossible at this date to say who is going to be doing the defiling. I worry about what is going to happen to the tiny mountain town of Dillard, the last town in northeast Georgia before you cross over into North Carolina, because there was a TV special the other night about how Dillard has caught the presidential fever and is being overrun by whitewater enthusiasts and souvenir hunters and people who have suddenly discovered the joys of living or at least of visiting Georgia life.

I worry most of all about St. Simons Island. We moved to St. Simons on Labor Day of 1972. It seemed the perfect place for a free-lance writer and his three children: four thousand residents; within bicycling range of anything important; one minute from the airport; three hundred miles from Atlanta; an hour's drive from Jacksonville and Savannah and the Okefenokee Swamp. The people on the island were, for the most part, natives who worked at the Georgia Burger House or changed mufflers or tended bar or ran fishing boats. The social center was the Binnacle Lounge.

Now, I am reading, St. Simons Island is the likely Summer White House of the Carter Administration. As a kid, Carter, who grew up two hundred miles to the west, probably spent some time on St. Simons. He probably likes the place, as I and thousands of other Georgians have liked it over the years. But now it, like the entire state of Georgia, has been thrust into a whole new orbit. Now St. Simons Island, Georgia, is important. It is, therefore, not worth visiting anymore.

The Promised Land

San Francisco

Nobody seemed to want me,
Or lend me a helping hand;
I'm on my way from 'Frisco,
I'm going back to Dixieland.
Jimmie Rodgers,
"Waitin' for a Train"

She appears, from the broad living-room window of the apartment we have occupied for nearly a year, like a crystalline toy city that some meticulous Swiss watchmaker whipped up in his spare time. From the staid old apartments of Pacific Heights you can see the San Francisco they feature on the picture postcards in the trashy tourist places down on Fisherman's Wharf—the bay; the Golden Gate Bridge; the brown, undulating hills of Marin County; Russian Hill; Nob Hill; the Coit Tower; sailboats and jet ferries and foreign tankers; Coast Guard helicopters—and the view can be absolutely breathtaking.

"How does she feel today?" my wife will say from the bedroom while I am standing in front of that window, holding a cup of coffee and checking out the city, and I might respond that she "has a bit of a hangover," or she is "feeling right sprightly," depending on whether it is the fog from the west or the sun from the east that happens to be running the show.

San Francisco. The City. Baghdad-by-the-Bay. "I Left My Heart in San Francisco." Songs all over the place. "You say 'Frisco one more time, pal, and I'll tell Herb Caen." What a sight she is, sparkling like diamonds at night and glimmering beside the Pacific most mornings, with her cable cars and dowdy Victorian mansions and surprising downtown parks and blue-haired dowagers and laid-back hippies and nude sunbathers and trolleys and rolling hills that appear to have been scrawled by a kindergartner. Grace and beauty. "L.A.," to paraphrase a poet, "comes screaming around a corner on two wheels and stops at the Taco Bell, while San Francisco sits in the cool of Trader Vic's and preens itself and talks about all those tacky other people."

So much for the good news. It will take a while longer to report the bad. The Golden Gate Bridge claimed its six hundred and first victim on the day after a gala celebrating its fortieth birthday. Last month some poor seventy-year-old fellow, sweeping out the lobby of a movie house downtown at three o'clock in the morning, was beaten to a bloody dead pulp with his own push broom. During the Christmas rush a trolley conductor folded under pressure and barreled down Market Street, refusing to unlock the doors for his frantic passengers, until the authorities managed to stop him at gunpoint.

Murder, suicide, alcoholism, snobbery, divorce, racism, provincialism. Those, once you get past the scenery, are the realities of San Francisco. For many decades it has been looked upon as the Promised Land by many people running from many things—homosexuals, bankrupts, the divorced, those who despaired—but for too many of those it has turned out to be a Paradise Lost. 'Frisco—I seem to think more kindly of the town when I call it " 'Frisco"—is like a cool and beautiful blonde in *haute couture* black who allows you to look her over, maybe even light her cigarette, and then kicks you in the groin. She is style over substance. A body without a soul.

"There are people," someone recently wrote, "who would kill to

be where Paul Hemphill was in the summer and fall of 1976."
Mainly they kill themselves, I thought, but I could understand the
theory. Last summer I went to San Francisco in order to recover
from my various aches—divorce, whiskey, ennui, no money—by
writing a daily newspaper column. I went in search of the Promised Land for the same reasons held by all of those before me, the
Okies and Chicanos and Filipinos and the rest, and for a while
California kept her promises. My lady came out from Tallahassee
and we married. The steady money eased other pains. I quit the
newspaper job and went back to free-lancing, my briar patch, and
a couple of books I was working on. We had fun, each of us, getting a fresh start in a new land.

A sort of restlessness toward California and San Francisco
began growing in me almost from the start, I think, but the piv-
otal moment came when I shuffled into the living room to watch
the inauguration of Jimmy Carter. After more than a century—a
century of being called "redneck" and "hillbilly" and worse—the
South finally had its own man in the White House. Most of my
life had been spent in the Deep South (nine different cities and
towns, at last count, ranging from Atlanta to little Dillard to the
Georgia mountains), but here I was now, the day we finally joined
the Union, sitting in a darkened room three thousand miles from
home, watching one of us right there on television as he became
the thirty-ninth president of the United States. When Carter took
his wife's hand and his daughter's hand and began to walk to the
White House—walk, by God—I cried, I cried hard.

There has been too much traveling. In forty-one years I have
lived in a lot of places and seen a lot of things, most of the time in
search of an elusive Promised Land. I'm not sure anymore that
there is such a place. If there is, maybe it was always right back
there at home, in Birmingham or Atlanta or Tallahassee or any of
those other stops we made during our apprenticeship while
changing buses and moving on to the next town. It is time to go
home now—home to the family and the old friends and the familiar streets and the children and the dogs—and see what is at the
beginning of the rainbow.

Home Again, Home Again

"*But, son, when are you going to quit all of this moving around and come on back home where you belong? It looks to me like you've had enough time to see all those other places.*"

My mother, Velma Nelson Hemphill

So we bolted and ran for home. The breaking away from our previous lives was done with. Our former spouses were doing what they chose to do. Now we were back home, after the wars, busy doing whatever we could to reconstruct our worlds. The tacky part was over with. Both of us had books to do. We had the child. We had the house in the old inner-city neighborhood. We had a simple and secure life. We seldom went out for dinner, preferring to have old friends come around for "supper" (generally meat loaf or pork chops or homemade vegetable soup and cornbread), and if you didn't say something nice about the kid, you got eighty-sixed. Downtown they had discos and forty-dollar dinners and the World's Tallest Hotel and crime and all of the other aches that American cities have contracted. But here we were, just a couple, trying to get along.

God. Does this sound boring. Man, nearing forty-four, cashes it in. I'm not saying that. What I am saying is—something I have been saying for years in writing classes—I don't believe anybody has any business writing a novel until he is past the age of forty. You must hurt and you must laugh and you must cry before you can write. You must have a kid die in your arms in a war and you must witness a pine box being "off-loaded" at the airport at dawn and you must see the pain of raising children and you must know the horrors of being in debt and you absolutely have to know that it is important to understand how to laugh before you will understand how to cry. Kiss the baby for me.

The Last Move

You always say, sitting there amid the paint buckets
and unemptied whiskey-store boxes and general
debris of everything you own, that this is it. This is the last move.
God knows I've said it enough. It might be cautious to say that I
have called some thirty places "home" in the last twenty years
since I flew my parents' coop and took an efficiency apartment
with a Murphy bed. Those places. All of those places. Fine new
apartments, drafty old houses, thirty-dollar-a-month rooming
houses, town houses, duplexes, barracks, basement apartments,
and even a sort of slaves' quarters in the courtyard of a country
house west of Paris. My wife, on the other hand, has lived in perhaps half a dozen places in her time. When I talk about how it
feels to be a gypsy she has no idea what I am talking about.

So now comes the latest—a modest old shotgun frame house on
the fringe of a downtown neighborhood in Atlanta—and once
again I find myself swearing that I have rented my last U-Haul.
I'm getting too old for this sort of thing, I say, rubbing my split
fingers and limping on one knee and trying to comb my hair with
a wrenched elbow and foraging for my favorite turtleneck and
muttering about the price the plumbers charged for pipes that
burst before we had even moved in. And why do I always pick

January for a move? And why do I love leaky old places? And why couldn't I get my Herbie Curbie (the wheeled curbside trash can used in Atlanta) for three weeks? And so on, into the cold winter nights, while rolling latex paint onto some perfectly awful phony paneling in the kitchen.

The answers are about as basic as the questions: January is a good month to get a deal, old places have what we call "charm," and the Sanitation Department surely must be busy this time of year. But there is a larger reason why we have chosen Inman Park—it could have been any number of other inner-city neighborhoods being brought back to life—and curiously it came to my mind the other night at Manuel's Tavern when Manuel Maloof hosted his annual memorial bash on the death date of Hubert Horatio Humphrey. The liberal Democrats who had known Humphrey were delivering informal testimonials to the man's humanity, and I regret that I did not give mine. "The legacy this man left for me," I said to Manuel late at night, "is that we have decided to put up or shut up. We've moved downtown. If we're going to play the liberal game, we're going to live it."

The panicky flight to the suburbs of America in recent years has consternated me no end. "Well," they say, "it's the schools. I'm no racist, understand, but I hear Bass High down there in Little Five Points is about ninety-percent nigger." You counter by saying that a school is a place to go and learn a little democracy and a tad of discipline and have some social life—that the real learning comes when a mother introduces her kids to books and a father gives them the benefit of his years out there—and you thoroughly enjoy needling them if they have so much goddamn pride in the superiority of their race, how come they're running wild-eyed to some double-car-garage enclave where only the mailmen and the yard men and the garbagemen aren't white Presbyterians. I also hate picket fences and $75,000 ticky-tacky boxes with built-in warped floors and cute little poodles named Phideaux and subdivisions with names like Kingsley Acres.

We try not to be smug about this—Committed Liberals Move to Inner City to Set Example—because the truth is that we already love our surroundings. On even the coldest afternoons I can hear the yelping of kids and the bouncing of basketballs on a school playground. The Little Five Points Pub and Manuel's Tavern are fine places to dawdle away dreary weekend afternoons. A major rapid-transit station is located two blocks away, so we can be downtown in six minutes. Our immediate neighbors include a seventy-two-year-old woman who moved into her house the very month I was born in 1936 and a pair of Ph.D. women and a raw-boned good old boy who once grabbed his towhead son on the sidewalk and said, "Come here, boy, or I'm gonna whup up on you." You've got one of each down here, and I call it democracy. The other day a photographer friend drove the two hours up from Augusta, the sleepy town on the South Carolina line where they hold the Masters Golf Tournament each year, and he parked his long, black Cadillac at the curb. He makes big money photographing the Masters and taking flattering studio portraits of the old-line blue bloods in Augusta. I noticed that his expensive automobile didn't have any hubcaps on the wheels, and I asked him why. "Are you kidding?" he said. "Every time we come to Atlanta we take 'em off and hang 'em in the garage." They don't call it "Hotlanna" for nothing.

Fast Freddie

Atlanta

The cost of living has risen so fast lately that nearly everybody has had to take an extra job to keep up. This is commonly known as "moonlighting," and the practice is so widespread that it is no longer an embarrassing situation. Some of the most important people in town are moonlighting. One of them is a very big department-store executive who is helping his little girl sell cookies for her Brownie troop in exchange for fifteen percent of the action. "September sales were up forty percent over August," he was saying the other day. "We came across a better brand of cookie."

Few people are immune to this rising cost of living, and it has been even more evident to Fast Freddie. Fast Freddie's business is hauling moonshine whiskey out of northeast Georgia into Atlanta, where nearly ninety percent of the homemade whiskey in the United States of America is sold. It used to be a profitable business, but it has become less profitable because operational costs, such as the price of new tires and fuel and sugar, have risen, and at the same time, the retailers of legal liquor have managed to keep their prices as low as before. So it has been very difficult lately for Fast Freddie to break even. "I thought about writing a letter to

Senator Talmadge," he was saying over the weekend, "but I figured he wouldn't want to get involved."

As a result of this, Fast Freddie, like almost everybody else, has been forced to take a second job. He has chosen the insurance business. This does not mean that Fast Freddie brings a load of whiskey into Atlanta on Friday night and spends all day Saturday and Sunday knocking on doors trying to convince people who make one hundred dollars a week that they should spend half of their income on various kinds of insurance. Fast Freddie, who is a man of strong ethics, regards that as dirty business. Instead, he looks around at the people who are collecting from insurance companies on trumped-up claims and he offers his services.

It was natural that Freddie should go into this type of business, because he is a talented man who happens to own a very versatile automobile. An automobile can be used like a meat cleaver, as Fast Freddie learned when he drove on dirt stock-car tracks from Jacksonville to Martinsville, but in the hands of Fast Freddie it becomes a scalpel. When he read about Junior Johnson, the stock-car driver, a few years ago in *Esquire* magazine, he consulted with Junior and went out and perfected what they call the "power slide." The power slide happens when you go fifty miles an hour and throw the car into a slide at full throttle, and all of a sudden you are going fifty miles an hour in the other direction. "If I'd know that when I was driving whiskey on them dirt roads up around Dawsonville," says Fast Freddie, "it'd saved me seven years and eight months and eleven days at the federal pen."

Now he is cashing in. The power slide is crucial to Fast Freddie's new job because what he does is hit people on the street just hard enough to put them into the hospital long enough to take a paid vacation or collect on accident insurance. His customers so far have included a corporate vice president who wanted to get away from his wife and a tavern owner being wiped out by daylight saving time's shorter nighttime hours.

"The trick is not to kill 'em," Fast Freddie was confiding. "It's all set up in advance. They walk across the street and I time it so I tap 'em in the middle of the power slide. It's really nothing but a little nudge. I coach 'em ahead of time about how to fall like those basketball players do when they're trying to fake a foul. If they listen to what I tell 'em, all they get out of it is a busted kneecap. Hitting 'em, that's easy. The trouble is with Herman."

You have to have a reliable witness in this operation, since Fast Freddie gets the hell out of there if he knows what is good for him, and the reliable witness is Herman the mechanic. Herman used to change tires and pour gas for Fast Freddie when Fast Freddie was driving stock cars. That was before everybody got concerned about so many moonshiners driving at family racetracks and passed a rule that said anybody with a record could not race. It nearly wiped out dirt-track stock-car racing in the South.

Now, when Fast Freddie is out on an insurance job he plants Herman across the street to witness the accident. Herman is supposed to be casually walking down the sidewalk when he sees this person get hit by an automobile. Then he is supposed to memorize the license plate and color and make of the nearest car, while Freddie power-slides back to the mountains, and halt the nearest car and help the wounded pedestrian until the cops come. If the client isn't hurt enough to draw blood, Herman takes out his Barlow knife and cuts the client's leg and, when the terrified motorist isn't looking, smears a respectable amount of blood on the bumper. Fast Freddie and Herman spent two months this winter drinking beer and riding Ferris wheels at the Florida resort in Panama City everybody calls the "Redneck Riviera."

The business was roaring until about a month ago. Fast Freddie's client was the owner of a haberdashery that was on the verge of bankruptcy—he was sitting on 238 iridescent men's suits, but everybody was going to blue jeans—so the client signed the contract, and Fast Freddie and Herman drove down to Atlanta on a Friday afternoon, at rush hour, to the appointed corner at Five Points, in dead-center downtown. Fast Freddie did his job perfectly. He swerved in on Peachtree, left the client screaming in the middle of the Peachtree-Marietta intersection, went into his power slide, and was headed north to the mountains before any witnesses could get his license-plate number.

Fast Freddie was still seething the other day when he was asked how the job turned out. "Nothing," he said, "not a goddamn cent. That dumb-ass Herman got drunk across the street in one of them fancy Atlanta bars while I was coaching the client and checking out the car, and by the time the cops got there he was stumbling around and couldn't even remember his name. So they threw him in the can for public drunkenness. Somebody told me my client's still in traction and looking for me."

The Burglar and
the Burglee

Atlanta

"I'll tell you the difference between moving into the inner city and moving out to Dunwoody," a friend of ours told us when we took over a creaking old house in Inman Park. "The first person to welcome you to the neighborhood in Dunwoody is a welcome-lady with a grin and a bowl of fruit. The first person to welcome you to Inman Park is a black cop with lines on his forehead and information about how to nail down your windows." We laughed knowingly, of course, and went about our business of painting and scraping and hammering and raking. We had always wanted to live in an old house close to town—felt it was our duty, in fact, as fairly young white Southern liberals—so we would accept whatever came. And so on the Saturday morning of our sixth week, feeling we owed ourselves a vacation, we loaded luggage into the car and took off for a weekend on St. Simons Island. The lamps and the plants and the cushions and the books were in place. Now we had a home.

When we returned thirty-six hours later, however, there was a shambles. Shattered glass was scattered about a rear door. The screen door had been popped open. Some nine hundred dollars' worth of goods was missing—everything from a cheap black-and-white television set to a K-Mart plant—and the drawers and the beds and the closets were disheveled. *How dare they?* was our thought as we called the man from THOR—the ultimate acronym, standing for "Target Hardening Opportunity Reduction"—and a host of other cops. We typed out a complete list of the articles missing, for the cops and for the insurance people, as a matter of routine. Catching a burglar is the old needle-in-a-haystack trick. It even happens to cops, as the man from THOR was saying: "It's probably a neighbor. Somebody in my neighborhood knew I had season's tickets to the Falcons games. On Sunday I came back from a game and I found I'd been moved. Everything was gone. You're lucky."

We are, in a sense, okay. Insurance will cover it. Some of the stuff wasn't exactly what we preferred to have, anyway, so now we can replace it. Some things are irreplaceable—grandmother's ageless stickpin and our wedding rings from previous marriages and the oil painting a friend did of country-music stars and the huge crocheted bedspread—but others can be covered in a minute. They are, after all, only things. Neither of us wants our life to be orchestrated by things. So the loss of possessions was not the point.

The larger point is that we have been violated. It is how a woman must feel on the subject of rape. A burglary represents a rape and an indignity. Somebody has come, uninvited, to look at your diary and smell your dirty clothes and see what you read and check on how much you drink and find out what you eat and learn how much you owe. On my desk was a letter from a publisher. On the bulletin board was the list of people who had come to our housewarming. On the bureau were photographs of our wedding ceremony and the latest bills from Master Charge. In our drawers were panties and prophylactics and dirty T-shirts and family heirlooms. "It is an outrage," said my wife. "Somebody has taken a look at your diary. Somebody out there knows all about you."

It doesn't happen only in the ghettos or in the inner-city neighborhoods. The smart burglar, in fact, goes out there to suburbia where the cars are bigger and the Oriental rugs aren't fake and the silverware is big-league. Twice before it had happened to me, and both times it took place in classier surroundings. Once, in Dunwoody, the two left-side tires were taken from my Volkswagen in the middle of the night ("Aw," said a bored cop answering the call, "Daddy buys these rich kids a dune buggy and leaves it up to them to get the tires"). The other time, in Tallahassee, my wardrobe of blue jeans and T-shirts and white socks was taken from a Laundromat while I was across the street buying cigarettes. But those cases were different because no one had looked into my life. No one had ripped my sheets from my bed or gone through my mail or rifled my drawers.

Now, of course, paranoia has set in. I don't care that the insurance will cover the loss. I have a prime suspect, and I intend to nail the scoundrel. New people were just moving into the neighborhood when it happened. It had to be somebody who saw us turning on our outside lights and locking doors and loading luggage at eight-thirty in the morning. It had to be a white (no black is going to take a country-music mural), and it had to be somebody outfitting a new apartment. So I keep peeking through the blinds and keeping an eye out, looking for a clue, and I do not like myself for feeling as I do these days. I even went over the list of the people we had invited to the housewarming—"It had to be somebody who knew you were going out of town," said the cop—and I feel particularly sheepish about that because these were our friends.

"A little bit of fear is a good thing because it keeps you on your toes," I was once told by the late Karl Wallenda, the tightrope walker, explaining why he never walked above a safety net. We certainly have "a little bit of fear" now. The house is becoming a prison, a place of "double-cylinder jimmy-proof" locks and nailed-down windows and solid-core doors and the rest of the burglary-proof gimmicks that represent America in the 1970s. We are antsy about staying out too late and we mistrust our neighbors and we are afraid to replace the stolen articles with anything of quality. I have a recurring fantasy, of late, that I somehow discover who did it and confront him with two choices: "I call the cops, or you give me fifteen minutes to gather all of the neighbors on the sidewalk to watch you bring back to my house—one at a time—all of the things you took from me." The one thing he could never return to me, though, is the dignity he took away.

The Girl in Gift Wrap

Atlanta

He worked in Men's Shoes and she worked in Gift Wrap, and he considered it the best part-time job he had ever had during any Christmas holiday. All day long, while he fitted feet to shoes and she wrapped Christmas gifts, they were no more than thirty feet apart. There were only thirty feet separating him and the most beautiful girl he had ever seen, and maybe it would have been better if he had a job on another floor, because the thought of being so close to her but never having spoken to her was driving him out of his mind.

The first thing he had noticed about her was the way she looked at the customers with her eyes. They were the most beautiful eyes in the world. They were dark blue, a very dark blue, with long, black eyelashes protecting them. He would go home every night remembering how she teased people by looking up at them through those long, black eyelashes. Her hair was black, too, a silken, shimmering black streaming down over her shoulders. And her face was soft and white, and her figure was like a ballet dancer's, and every day she wore baby blue or desert tan or mint green to promote all of this to the fullest. Here he was, working thirty feet away, and he did not know how much longer he could stand being so close, yet so far away. It really was a wonderfully painful kind of job, being in Men's Shoes while she was in Gift Wrap.

And now it was the last week before Christmas. He knew he was going to have to find some way to talk to her before they both went back to school, if she went to school at all, and he did not know how he was going to do it.

Once, he thought he was in love with a girl in high school. That was his senior year. All year long he tried to sit near her and her dates during the football and basketball games, and he even prayed he would be in the same classes with her. She had a lot of dates, and this discouraged him, so he never got around to asking her for a date. It wasn't until he had graduated and gone to college that he learned why she had been so popular, and because he had not dreamed she was that kind of girl, that made him feel even more awkward.

But now the Christmas holidays were almost over. The crowds of shoppers were thinning. Those who came now were men buying at the last minute for their wives. There were only three more shopping days until Christmas. Three more days to do something. And he chose to make his move on her coffee break.

The snack bar where she always went for her break was not crowded. That would make it easier for him. He had waited for her to leave, and then he had followed her, and when she took one of the stools at the counter he took another, leaving one stool between them, and after their snacks had come, he cleared his throat and said. "Well, it's almost over now."

"Yes, and I hope I never see another package," she said. "I work in Gift Wrap."

"I know. I work in Men's Shoes. Next to you," he said. She seemed friendly enough. And her eyes really were beautiful.

"Ah, do you go to school?" he asked her.

"No. I'm just trying to make some money for Christmas."

"Yeah. Me, too. I'm in college."

"What are you studying?"

"Engineering. I'm going to be an engineer."

"That's wonderful. That's a good profession, isn't it?"

"It sure is," he said, looking into her beautiful blue eyes.

She said, "What's Santa Claus going to bring you for Christmas?" She laughed, a very nice laugh, when she said it.

"Oh, I don't know. Clothes, I guess. How about you?"

She answered so quickly and easily and pleasantly. That is what made it hurt. "An engagement ring," she said.

"Oh," he said. And he went back to Men's Shoes, and she to Gift Wrap. She was only thirty feet away. There were three miserable days to go.

A Certain Satisfaction

Atlanta

When they are young it does not matter. They need money and they want something better than standing behind a lunch counter and they are pretty in a way, and so they take a job as an "exotic." They take their clothes off in nightclubs. They take their clothes off in New York City and they take their clothes off in Opelika, Alabama. Sometimes the money is little better than what the cocktail waitresses on the floor make. They learn to take abuse from the men in the audience. Then the years pile up and the face and the body begin to show it, and when they are forty-five there is nowhere else to turn. "I was in show business," they can say. Everybody knows they used to take their clothes off.

She had flown in from Los Angeles at six o'clock in the morning to begin a one-month stand at a place in Atlanta called the Gypsy Room. She had not been to sleep all day. Her musical arrangements had been lost in St. Joseph, Missouri, of all places, so she had come down to the Gypsy early to rehearse with the band. And now it was almost nine at night and the place was starting to fill up, and she sat at one of the tables in the back of the room.

"A stripper gets a certain satisfaction out of working, just like any other entertainer," she was saying. "Certainly it's not sexual satisfaction. It's the same as for a singer. You want people to appreciate you. You dress up and fix yourself up nice, and while you're performing you like for them to make you think you're very pretty. It's different, of course, when you wake up in the morning. You're tired and you don't look as pretty as you thought you did the night before, and you're afraid to go out until it's dark. I never liked hotel lobbies. You feel like everybody's staring at you."

She is billed as "Kalantan, the Heavenly Body," but her real name is Mary and she is married to the actor John Bromfield. She has been a stripper for twenty-one years. In daylight, probably, you might be able to tell. But under soft lights, with the false eyelashes and the makeup on, and the band playing and the waitresses pouring drinks, not too many seem to notice. Besides, she is one of the best. She has outlasted most of them and still draws the big crowds and the big money.

"So now you've started singing, too?" somebody said.

"Since the last time I was here. A few months."

"Had you sung before? I mean, years ago?"

She said, "No, but I felt like I had to do it. Sometimes I'm not very good. The voice just won't come, you know. Then, other times, I'm not bad at all. It's just something I had to do. I think it adds to the performance."

Sitting at the table with her were three good friends. One of them was a husky businessman from California named Keith, who has a place on the beach next to the Bromfields and was in Atlanta "selling cotton to Southerners." The couple, a young man named Jeff and his wife, always have her stay with them when she is playing in Atlanta. All of them had come to see her first show.

"She's my couturiere," Kalantan said, nodding toward Jeff's wife.

"Hey, that's some word."

Jeff's wife smiled. "It means I make the clothes you don't wear. What'll it be tonight?"

"The black. Of course."

"Ummmmm. Wonderful. I can't wait."

Keith said, "Where's John?"

"The poor dear. In New York, working on a show. He's really having a hard time."

"We'll have to go fishing when we all get back."

"Fishing, yes," Kalantan said. "Eating, no. I've got to recover from the holidays. I'm getting fat."

"That'll be the day."

It was not the sort of conversation the man in the audience would have expected. Monday night is a lousy night all over town, but the Gypsy Room was going to do well. There would be four girls, an off-color emcee, and then the star, Kalantan. They would not have expected Kalantan to be talking about fishing and her husband and overeating.

The girl on the stage now looked to be no more than nineteen years old. She was "Adorable Eileen," and there was sweet innocence on her face as she awkwardly went about the business of taking off her clothes. Kalantan watched her critically for a few minutes and then excused herself to go backstage to prepare for her act. You wonder where both of them will be twenty-one years from now.

Birthing Babies

Atlanta

Entangled in each other's arms the other night, with the television blinking and the sirens crying and the yard dogs snarling, we talked about it. She is thirty-four and I am forty-two. I had three children in my first marriage and she had none. A woman, they say, shouldn't take the chance of giving birth once she reaches thirty-five. Each of us had gone for a complete medical checkup, and each of us had been assured that the physical parts were working all right. "There is no reason why you can't have a perfectly normal baby," her doctor told her. My doctor had told me, "I figure you'll still be around for high-school graduation when you're sixty." So here we were, we two middle-agers, bundling late at night and whispering about a possibility that we knew to be anything but simple.

"It's probably selfish," she said.

"I know," I said.

"I want to know what it's like."

"Me, too. And I say it's good."

"It'll change our lives. You know that."

"Do I ever. I've changed diapers in my time. Plenty."

"I might get fat."

"For a good cause."

And so we played games with genealogy. We made up names. It had to be Paul if a boy (for me and for her father) and Martha if a girl (for her mother). Paul, or Paulie? Martha, or Martie? Pink, or blue? Private school, or public? Auburn, or Radcliffe? Housewife or writer or truck driver or jock or executive or rock singer? It didn't really matter much at the time. The only thing certain was that he/she would occupy what is now the guest room.

This sounds like a soap opera, of course, and maybe it is. People aren't having babies as they used to. You've got your committed Catholics and your Asians and your Africans and your poor people who don't know what birth control means—these, generally, are the people who are throwing askew all of the statistics about per capita births in the world these days—but the movement in the seventies has been toward "family planning." Americans, particularly, are "into" such "philosophies" as "personal growth" and "gaining space" and "doing your own thing." This has led to a remarkable decline in the birth rate. Except in rural Kansas and in big-city ghettos, which are more alike than they would like to admit, you don't see "extended family" so much these days: three generations living together under the same roof, sharing the cooking and the cleaning and the agonies. The new American may be what we experienced in a year of living in California. They are a professional couple, with separate careers, living in a high-rise apartment and sharing the duties around the place—throwing white-wine parties and taking the subways and working in downtown skyscrapers and reading *The New York Times* on Sunday mornings—and they are a comfortable distance away from falling out of bed at three o'clock in the morning to burp the baby and prepare a formula. Back home in Atlanta, after a year of living like this in California, a thought occurred to me while wandering around a shopping center one day. *Who are all of these pregnant women?* I hadn't seen one in a year.

There is something sadistic about wanting to make a baby. The price one pays is horrendous, on the one hand (late nights, nursing, bills, angers, impositions in general), but the glories are many (cuddling, mimicking, watching them grow). It is an *impasse.* I remember the feeling I had at the birth of my first one just as vividly as I remember the feeling I had when my second one got his foot caught in the revolving door of a supermarket. You win some, with babies, and you lose some. "Beware of children," says a friend, "for they will sell you out."

So why, at our age, do we want a kid? I suppose it is because parenting, along with sex and hunger, is one of our most basic instincts. *Birds do it, bees do it. . . .* We want, selfishly, to procreate. The success of the book and the movie versions of *Roots* was no accident. We have a deep craving to extend ourselves beyond our time. We want to be remembered. If I can't be remembered through my own work, I can be remembered, by God, through the works of my sons and daughters. Thus, if it is a boy, his name shall be Paul Hemphill.

One of the heroes of my youth was a baseball player by the name of Nellie Fox. His real name was Jacob Nelson Fox and he played second base for the Chicago White Sox in the 1950s and early '60s. I wanted to be a professional baseball player at the time, and Nellie, like me, was a small infielder who made it on hustle and desire and a little talent. I was about fifteen years old when my parents told me that my name, for the first week of my life, was James Nelson Hemphill. They changed it to Paul James Hemphill, Jr., when my mother finally convinced my father that it wasn't all that selfish to make me a "Junior." I kept thinking, as they told me the story, that I could have been Nellie Hemphill. Just like my idol. Nellie. I sulked for three weeks. There has to be a moral here, somewhere, about birthing babies.

The Oldest Game

Atlanta

It was nine o'clock in the morning when Aggie heard the knock on her door. Aggie is close to fifty-five years old, and she is big enough to make Ella Fitzgerald look like a midget. She takes in boarders to help pay bills. She got out of bed and opened the door and there was this old fellow with gray hair and three gold teeth.

The man said he was with the construction crew down the street and had been sent by the boss man to see if she would be interested in taking in some boarders. A lot of the men had come from out of town for the job, he had told her, and they needed a place to stay. Aggie's eyes lighted up and she said yes. Then the skinny guy in the straw hat and alligator loafers joined them on the porch, and that was when Aggie began learning how they play the oldest game.

"What you got in them envelopes?" Aggie said.

"Well, I might as well tell both of y'all about it," said the one with the gold teeth. "I found me a whole lot of money up the street in the phone booth, and I don't know what to do with it."

"Lemme see," Aggie said.

The man reached into one of the two white envelopes he was carrying, and he pulled out a thick wad of green bills. The one on the outside looked like a thousand dollar bill to Aggie. She was scared.

"What you gonna do with it?" she said.

"Let's go inside so nobody can hear us," said one of them.

So Aggie looked both ways and quickly showed the two men into her house. And the three of them sat and talked about what they were going to do about the money. The one in the straw hat and the loafers excused himself to go check on the rest of the money. When he came back he had it all.

"Ain't no tellin' how much is in here," he said.

"What we gonna do?" Aggie pleaded.

"First off," the other man said, "I think we oughta tell the boss man exactly what happened. He oughta know what's right." And he sent the skinny one to see the boss man. He was back very soon. Aggie and the older man sat breathlessly to hear what the boss had advised them to do about the money.

"He says we ought to keep it," the man told them. "He says if you turn it over to the police, all they'll do is keep it. He says we ought to just keep it and divide it up amongst ourselves."

"I'm afraid," Aggie said. "It's somebody else's money."

And one of the men said, "You heard what the boss man told us. He ought to know."

"Something else the boss man said, too."

"What's that?"

"He says before we go splitting money up with folks we don't know, we ought to find out if they're reliable."

"How we gonna find out?"

"Boss man says everybody ought to put up some of their own money just to show they can be counted on."

The skinny one with the straw hat reached into his pocket and pulled out a huge roll of bills. The one on the outside looked like a hundred-dollar bill. He gave the roll to the big man with the gold teeth. Then the big man, the one who found the money, asked Aggie how much she could put in the pot. She said she could get $850 out of her account at the bank. The big man said that sure ought to prove she was reliable, and if she did that he would give Aggie and the little man nine thousand apiece.

And now Aggie was on fire. Nine thousand dollars! The big man said he had to go and do something and he would take the money with him. Aggie let the skinny man drive her car, and together they went to the bank.

Aggie drew out her $850 and took it back to the car. She gave it to the skinny man, and he put it in a brown envelope. They talked for a few minutes. The man told Aggie that now all she had to do was walk into the drugstore over there and look for a man who would be identified by the code name "Number Five." And he gave her a brown envelope.

"That's your eight hundred fifty," he said. "You show it to Number Five and then he'll give you your nine thousand dollars."

The skinny man in the straw hat got out of the car and said good-bye to Aggie. And Aggie walked into the drugstore, looking for Number Five. She waited for half an hour. Finally Aggie did the smartest thing she had done all day. She looked inside the brown envelope. And she had the cops on the phone in a matter of minutes. In the envelope, folded neatly as possible, were two rolls of newspaper.

Boosting Betty

Atlanta

L ast week, with barely forty shopping days left, the people who operate department stores throughout Georgia began to crank up for the Christmas-shopping season. This does not mean they started stocking their electric can openers, because most of that had already been done. This does not mean they began preparing their Christmas displays, either, because that is usually accomplished well in advance. What the retailers of Georgia were doing last week was setting up their defenses against people who believe it is poor planning to go into the red for Christmas gifts. These infiltrators are commonly known as shoplifters, or "boosters."

The occasion was a meeting of more than one hundred members of the Georgia Retail Association at the Dinkler Plaza Hotel in downtown Atlanta. Sitting in orderly rows of metal folding chairs in a rooftop meeting room, the retailers saw a twenty-minute color film about how shoplifters operate and then listened to Lt. W. K. Perry, of the Atlanta Police Department's larceny squad.

"In a recent report the FBI reported that shoplifting is fast becoming the top form of larceny," said Lieutenant Perry. "It has increased by ninety-three percent over the last five years. Shoplifters now account for a one- to one-and-a-half-percent loss in your net sales. First we will show the film, so you can see real criminals in action."

It was a very good film. "One out of every sixty people who enter your store will steal," the narrator said. He said the best days for shoplifters are Friday and Saturday, and the best hours are the opening, closing, and lunch hours, because that is when store employees drop their guard. He added that ten percent of the shoplifting is done by professionals, and eighty-five percent is done by housewives. The footage showed boosters in action, using bulky coats and fake packages and ordinary shopping bags to take merchandise out of the store. "One colored female told us the largest item she had ever taken was a typewriter," Lieutenant Perry said after the film. "She 'legged' it, or stuck it between her legs and walked out with it."

Boosting Betty seemed very interested when she heard about the retailers' meeting the next day. "Flattered" is a better word for how she felt, because Boosting Betty is highly respected by her neighbors as one of the all-time-great Christmas shoppers. Boosting Betty will go about two hundred pounds, and she wears a big coat, anyway, and she has already made out her shopping list.

"It's my favorite time of year," she was saying.

"The woman who took the typewriter: Was that you?"

"Lawd, no. Me and the po-leeces ain't never met."

"But what if you do? What if they catch you?"

"They tells me that's some nice Christmas dinner they serves down at the po-leece station," said Boosting Betty.

The most successful boosters use an accomplice. The accomplice can be used as a lookout or to divert attention while the booster goes about selecting merchandise. Boosting Betty's accomplice is her son, Melvin, who is eight years old now and is about to hit his peak after two years' experience. Melvin's job is to create a disturbance, something the other people on the block say he comes by naturally. They will enter a store, Boosting Betty and Melvin, and while his mother checks the exits and the general layout and makes up her mind what she wants, Melvin will mind his manners. Then when Boosting Betty begins stuffing merchandise between her legs and under her coat, Melvin will go into his act. He will take a toy airplane and throw it at a saleswoman, or pedal a tricycle into the ladies' room. He will be so bad that every salesperson in the area will leave his post and go after Melvin. By this time Boosting Betty has usually finished her chores, but if she needs more time, Melvin will fall to the floor and scream that somebody hit him. They are so glad to see Boosting Betty come get her kid and drag him out of the store that they never know what hit them.

"He's such a good boy," Boosting Betty was saying. "Melvin, ain't you gonna show your new trick?"

Obediently, Melvin threw himself on the floor and began flailing himself back and forth. He beat on the floor with his fists, gagged, rolled his eyes, and kicked the wall. He did not stop until his mother said, "Fine, boy, real fine."

"What was that?" Boosting Betty was asked.

"Epileptic seizure," she said. "The poor boy's got a history of it."

End of the Rainbow

Atlanta

It is nearly fifty years since they were married in a ceremony held on the stage of the Ritz Theatre, between movies, in Birmingham, Alabama. They were the children of the Depression—both had been forced to drop out of high school to help their families survive—and they had been surprised to learn they had won the grim little downtown movie house's quest for the "Perfect Couple." About the only thing anybody had in Birmingham in those days was black lungs and dirty fingernails. So they answered the newspaper ad and won the right to be married onstage at the Ritz—included in the package was a wedding ring for the bride presented by a balding jeweler named Friedman—and before the lights went down for the second movie of the evening at the Ritz, they were already hustling off, with lust in their hearts and bodies, for a free wedding night in the honeymoon suite at the Thomas Jefferson Hotel, two blocks away. They had to walk it.

Each was twenty years old then, and times were hard. She stayed at home and gave birth to two children while he lurched out at dawn every day of the week to scratch up bread and milk. He worked at her father's coal mine and served as a "newsbutch" on the daily excursion train to Chattanooga and then tried his own one-man coal-mine operation for a while. The days began at five A.M. and ended toward midnight. Sometimes he earned twenty-five dollars a week. They paid a black maid named Louvenia fifty cents a day to help with the first child and with the bleak little house they rented in a blue-collar neighborhood of Birmingham. There were people in the Hamptons, up on Long Island, who played tennis and worked on suntans and were not aware that the country was in an economic depression. Maybe the people of Birmingham didn't realize there was a depression, either, because this was the only way of life they had ever known. People in the South didn't eat grits and cornbread because they necessarily liked it. They ate grits and cornbread because it was there.

So the years rolled along. One morning around the time of Pearl Harbor there came a fierce sawing and hammering noise from the backyard. He was making "sideboards" for his trailer and converting his coal truck. "There's gonna be a lot of stuff needs hauling," he told his young son, "and I'm gonna help 'em out." He spent the war years running all over the country with war matériel—helmets, explosives, machine guns, uniforms—and he was paid well for his endless nights on the road. When the war was over he bought his first house in three payments and then bought the "seventy-eighth new Dodge automobile sold in Birmingham since the war."

Nobody in his family had been able to afford college—his father, who had run a country store in upper-middle Tennessee, had died when he was eight—and when his son became eighteen it was time to ponder the possibility of having a college graduate in the family. So she took a job with Social Security and he continued his long-distance trucking, and the boy, after fooling around with dreams of playing professional baseball, entered college. Four years later the daughter, four years younger, also graduated. Both represented a break in the family cycle. The mother and the father were proud. "I took a correspondence course once, but I had to quit when the Injuns shot the Pony Express rider," the old man took to saying later, trying for a quick laugh, but the shine in his eyes reflected his disappointments as well as his happiness.

And now, nearly a half a century since that night of the free wedding on the stage of a movie house in Birmingham, Velma Rebecca and Paul James Hemphill, Sr., are testing retirement in a trailer park on the fringes of Lakeland in central Florida. They are in their late sixties. It is a nice trailer, with a screened porch and a car port, and it cost them $4500 (fully furnished) and there is only a $56-a-month maintenance charge for the land and the utilities. They watch the money closely, in the manner of those who had to get by during the Depression (he drives supermarket managers crazy by buying huge loads of the advertising-loss-leader specials and eschewing the overpriced steaks), and she plays bridge with other blue-haired retirees on the screened porch while he takes a beer and meanders down to the dock to dangle his feet and toss bread to the four-foot alligator that is just as much a citizen of the Lake Bonny Mobile Homes Trailer Court as anyone else.

It was occurring to me, as my mother poured some champagne into Styrofoam cups for me and my wife during our visit over the holidays at what they fiercely insist on calling their "mobile home," how glibly simple it has always been to ridicule people who retire to trailer camps in Florida. About one out of seven people in Florida are retirees. They fish, sleep late, play bridge, wear Bermuda shorts and double-knit leisure suits and golf caps, stretch their Social Security dollars, fall asleep at the television set, vote Republican, and look at pictures of their grandchildren. "Yeah," says my old man, "now that I'm *retarded*—that's what the government's calling me now, you know, *'retarded'*—I don't hardly know what to do with myself. I keep looking for the *partial post* to bring me something in the mail. . . ." She misses her friends at the church in Birmingham and he, a man who spent most of his life on the road, thinks about hiring out at an orange grove two blocks away. This is the end of their rainbow. They deserve to see it. I, their firstborn, can hardly remember what it looks like.

Father, 43,
Does It Again

Atlanta

The first kid came sixteen years ago, two years into the first marriage, and it took forty-eight hours in the labor room ("Yeah, I unnerstan' they had to *seduce* labor," said a fat sportswriter friend) before Elisabeth Warren Hemphill was introduced to the world. David, the second, came two years later and was so impatient they had to shove a wheelchair under his mother and take the express elevator to the delivery room in order to catch him in time. Molly, the third, came under what the people at Ob-Gyn called "normal circumstances." What the obstetricians of that time did, to be poetic about it, was take the mother and more or less sledgehammer her, as cowboys do when they hit cattle between the eyes to drive them through the chutes. "Go off to a bar and leave the number," they would tell me, the father, "and we'll call you to tell you whether it's a boy or a girl." It was either that or the obscenity of sitting in the Father's Waiting Room, where a voice would boom out now and then from a public-address system—"Will Mister J. Thomas Warrenton please pick up the red phone on the wall"—and everybody would stop talking, and then the poor devil who had been flaked out on a Naugahyde sofa for six hours while his wife was in there yelling and birthing would grab the phone and hear a doctor say, "It's a girl and she's healthy and her mom is all right," and he would drop the phone and say something like "Whooo-pee" and start throwing cigars around to the other poor devils. And then the others would lie back in agony and wonder if their name was the next to be called. That—the waiting, the impersonality of it all, the *not being involved*—was the worst part of being a father.

And then I, father of three, got divorced. There was the wandering for three or four years—one girl friend was a blond tennis player who has warm memories of the Master Race; another was a brunette from Montgomery who loved shooting pool at three A.M.; another was a *Gone with the Wind* honey from south Alabama who figured I should pay for her cab fare if I was going to have her body—until finally I met the one I wanted to take up with. She was nearly ten years younger than I. She had been married for a decade to a man who simply didn't want to have children. I loved children, it was clear, but I had been stripped of them. She wanted the experience of having a child. So we married and we plotted the birth of the child who would cement our marriage. And we began attending Lamaze classes.

Lamaze, essentially, is a system in which the mother-to-be and the father-to-be learn how to go through what they call "natural childbirth." What it means is that the father will be there in the delivery room—no more of those ghastly intercom announcements—to witness the birth. The mother, at least until the pain gets to be too bad, will be alert. It is a sharing. At the seven Lamaze classes we attended there was an emphasis on breathing exercises, for father and mother, and there were films showing exactly what was going to happen.

They can't really show you or tell you what is going to happen. It is something you really can't talk about. We were getting ready to go out to a dinner party on a Saturday night. At eight o'clock Susan was walking from the bedroom to her bath, to make up her face, when her water broke. I told her to lie back on the bed. In an hour the pains came. I called the doctor. He said everything was on schedule, even though the baby was due three weeks later, and that we should check into the hospital. We checked in around ten-thirty at night. By dawn they had given her slight medication and she was in the delivery room and they were putting a gown and mask on me and I was joining her.

People ask me, "Hemphill, haven't you done your part for world population? What the hell is this? You're forty-three and you've already got three kids. What're you doing this for?" I wondered myself, because kids can bring one a lot of pain, and they sure as hell cost money. But I am here to tell those people, and the ones who have never experienced the joys and angers and expenses and frustrations of birthing children, about the highest high that one can ever have. At exactly six-thirty on the last Sunday morning of January, 1979, with Ma in her stirrups and Pa in his cap, the head of Martha Farran Hemphill popped out into the world. There was a mirror hanging from the ceiling. We saw this furry head come out of this bloody crotch, the doctor imploring the mother to "push one more time," and we sat there and looked up at the mirror and Susan rolled out words that I will never forget. They were simple words, spoken slowly and evenly, and when I heard them I felt as though I were hearing the Old Testament capsulized into three words. "Oh, Paul, *look*," she said. I stood up and threw my arms out like Rocky in the movie and, to the embarrassment of all, shouted, "That's just about the goddamnedest thing I'll ever see in my life." Susan, the mother, told me to shut up and sit down and don't go around town bragging.